Building
Trust
at the
Speed of Change

Building
Trust
at the
Speed of Change

The Power of the
Relationship-Based
Corporation

Edward M. Marshall

American Management Association

New York • Atlanta • Boston • Chicago • Kansas City • San Francisco • Washington, D.C.
Brussels • Mexico City • Tokyo • Toronto

This publication is designed to provide accurate and authoritative information in regard to the subject matter covered. It is sold with the understanding that the publisher is not engaged in rendering legal, accounting, or other professional service. If legal advice or other expert assistance is required, the services of a competent professional person should be sought.

Library of Congress Cataloging-in-Publication Data

Marshall, Edward M.
    Building trust at the speed of change : the power of the
relationship-based corporation / Edward M. Marshall.
        p.   cm.
    Includes bibliographical references and index.
    ISBN 0-8144-0478-2
    1. Industrial management.   2. Work ethic.   3. Cooperativeness.
4. Management.   I. Title.
HD30.5.M367   1999
    658.4'06—dc21   99–34449
                                                                CIP

Printing number

10 9 8 7 6 5 4 3 2 1

Contents

Preface

"Relationships without trust are merely transactions. Speed without trust cannot be sustained."

In the legend of John Henry, there was a contest, between the strongest pile driver on the railways and a steam-powered engine, to see who could lay down rail the fastest. With his muscles bulging and sweat pouring off his brow, John Henry showed his determination, grit, and heart as he tried to save the jobs of his fellow workers by demonstrating that people were stronger than machines. John Henry won the initial race, but then his heart gave out. The machine took over.

Fast-forward to the 1990s, when Garry Kasparov was pitted against IBM's "Deep Blue" computer in a world-class chess competition. Again the determination, intelligence, and heart of the world's leading chess champion was pitted against a machine. Again the machine won, and while Kasparpov's heart did not fail, our belief that machines will eventually outstrip human capacity took a symbolic leap forward.

The Need to Evolve

This classic struggle between man and machine, as well as the never-ending advance of technology, has also been evident in the evolution of human organization, and particularly the business organization. Like John Henry and Garry Kasparov, the workforce has the intelligence, resolve, and heart to meet the challenges of the market head on. However, our leading and managing philosophies, let alone our organizational systems, have not evolved as quickly as needed to meet the challenges of speed that technology throws at us daily.

We have no choice but to change, though we resist it daily. At the same time, we know that if we do not alter the ways in which we work together, and do so quickly, the inexorable pressures of the market and the demands for more speed will push our businesses out of the competitive picture.

We are beginning to see the type of workplace we need so that we can meet these pressures. To do so, however, we must be willing to alter the fundamental premises upon which we have led and managed people for the last century. This book is about that choice and the next stage in the evolution of the business organization. It is about the choices we need to make if we are to honor our workforce with the trust they must have to succeed, while we honor our customers with the speed and quality they require. It is not a zero-sum game. We *can* have both trust and speed. But we must be very clear about the sequence: We must build trust *first*, then we can successfully meet the challenges of speed.

Machines vs. People

In recent business history, it was Frederick Winslow Taylor who, in the early 1900s, went around plants with a stopwatch, conducting time and motion studies to see how management might get people to work more efficiently—like machines. A number of years later, it was Douglas McGregor's turn to help us understand that the human heart has a place at work, and that when people are given attention and support, they produce more. In business, however, the assembly line won over the advocates of more heart in the workplace.

The machine has consistently been the metaphor, even the model, for how we believe we should organize ourselves in business. We have consistently assumed, and demonstrated over time, that the mechanistic approach to work is more efficient and more productive. When the increased speed of the machine was coupled with the power of a chain of command and specialized jobs, we found we could outstrip the competition.

The human side of enterprise seems always to have been a secondary consideration. Even today, those theorists, behavioral scientists, and business leaders who have articulated the need to focus on the value of people are criticized as being too soft and not sufficiently concerned with the bottom line. As companies have struggled to deal with the realities of mergers, increased global competition, and the speed of change, they have merely revived the strategies of the past. These strategies focus on the bottom line vs. a balanced ledger, the application of power rather than principle, and the use of technical rather than people solutions. Why have we drawn these lines so starkly?

This classic struggle between people and machines has even been played out in the world of change management and organizational development. Here, the prevailing paradigm is to use techniques and organizational changes to produce short-term, bottom-line improvements. In these methodologies, the workforce is often viewed as a cost and liability rather than a resource or intellectual asset. To meet the competitive challenges of cost and speed, we have convinced ourselves that the only way to survive is to downsize, reengineer, or restructure millions of people out of their jobs. In some instances, this approach was justified in order to survive. What we are learning, however, is that companies cannot *save* their way to prosperity. Maybe we really believed these approaches were right and that's why we did not look for other methods. Or maybe we have been looking for a new approach but could not find it. This book presents a new approach that has worked, and that treats the workforce as an asset and resource in the change process. At the end of the day, it is only the character, will, and discipline of our workforce that will make the short- or long-term difference.

The Millennium Challenge

In this millennium that is coming to a close, with all of its uncertainty and opportunity, we once again face the question of what will be preeminent in our businesses—technology or people? With the twilight of the industrial age and the rise of an information age, we continue to grapple with how best to meet these challenges, whether it is with power or principle. Yet we remain entangled in the paradigms of the past. We seem to be clinging tenaciously to the deck railings of the organizational *Titanic* as its basic assumptions slowly sink beneath the sea. Many of us still believe there is little or no alternative.

What adds to the sense of desperation is the nonstop speed of the market, the unrelenting challenges of global competition, and the deluge of data. The intensity is only increasing, and our response is to try to go faster. We scan the horizon for more technological solutions, when our greatest resource is right in front of our eyes. That resource is the commitment, competence, and intelligence of our workforce. How much longer can we afford to overlook their preeminent role as a strategic asset in outstripping the competition?

The demise of the command and control approach to business is at hand. Unlike the buggy-whip makers of old who failed to see the future coming, however, we can see that a new day is dawning. In our future, the primary differentiater among companies will be how they value their greatest asset—their workforce—and how they leverage that asset to produce greater quality and speed.

We Do Have a Choice

We do have a choice. We must learn that increasing our speed has very little to do with going faster. We get greater speed by trusting the people we work with and by creating workplaces that nurture that trust. We can outstrip any competitor and win any global challenge if we learn how to tap into the potential of our workforce, a resource that is hidden from our view by their fear. To do so, however, we must be willing to move beyond the past, to allow our approach to evolve into one of leading and managing businesses, to move from a position based on fear and compliance to one based on trust, relationships, and collaboration. This is the most significant business challenge we face today.

We have at least three conscious choices to make. The first choice is to let go of the past, to realize that tradition is tradition, and that those who fail to learn from the past are doomed to repeat those mistakes. The second choice is one of acceptance.

We need to accept the reality that people are still the most critical asset and variable in the success of a business. Without them, there is no ability to produce. Without their energy, enthusiasm, pride, and dignity, we will not excel at anything. Our third choice is to accept that what people want and need at work is to be trusted, respected, honored, and acknowledged. All things being equal, the companies that succeed in the information age will be those that move beyond thinking about labor as a cost and see the workforce as intellectual capital.

Given these choices, the type of business organization that will be the most effective and productive, let alone the fastest, will be the one that understands how to mobilize the power of trust-based relationships in the workplace. This view of the relationship between employees and machines recognizes that in the Knowledge Era, the scales of organization must be tipped in favor of the human side of business.

My Journey

In 1995, when my book *Transforming the Way We Work: The Power of the Collaborative Workplace* was published by AMACOM, I was profoundly touched by the responsive chord it struck with so many people. There was a growing belief among businesspeople that collaboration was this new approach to the workplace, and that all we needed to do was find a way to create it. Many tried. Some succeeded. Most failed. When the approach was given a chance, it flourished in teams, offices, and even departments. When it was allowed to work, the power of authentic collaboration transformed people's lives, work relationships, and business results. But when this approach was seen as a threat, the auto-immune systems of power and bureaucracy kicked in, and in many instances collaboration became just another program of the month.

What was missing? Why was collaboration not taking the business world by storm? There had to be a reason. In my personal journey over the last several years, working with thousands of people wanting to find a new way to work, wanting to beat the challenge of speed, I found that perhaps the focus needed to shift—from a philosophical position to one based on what people really need and want at work.

What was missing was an emphasis on trust and relationship, and on the corporate system to support it, while simultaneously focusing on meeting customer needs. I learned that when we are able to look behind the faces of fear and listen to people's hearts speak, there is an incredible energy and vitality in their work, their company, and their commitments to each other. Our job as leaders and managers, I then concluded, is to create a relationship-based workplace that will strip away that fear, release that energy, focus more on the customer, and build a work culture that will sustain that energy over time. Only in this way will we achieve the speed we need.

What was missing has always been there—right in front of us. All we have to do is look.

Dedicated to You

So I dedicate this book to honor all of you who have seen the future and have taken risks to evolve your organizations into ones based on trust and on honoring the dignity of the workforce. For you, this book is a next step in the evolutionary process, an expanded framework for integrating the core values of trust-based relationships into every aspect of the workplace.

This book is also written for all those people who believe the workforce is an organization's critical asset, but who may be losing hope that others share this belief. For you, the framework and experiences presented here are an affirmation of your conviction; indeed, there *are* people and businesses that share your view and that are practicing that conviction.

I also write this book to honor those of you who have weathered the storms of organizational change, the many "programs of the month," and who have hoped that there is still another way to transform your workplace into one based on trust and mutual respect. For you, this book is a restatement of your hopes for an organization that works and a collaborative change methodology that will get you there.

Finally, I write this book out of respect for all those people in businesses, whether large or small, in all parts of this country, who have practiced or are trying to practice the art of collaboration, and have either succeeded or have encountered serious obstacles. This book is intended to reinforce your commitment. You are headed in the right direction. Honor your principles and maintain your commitments. Be patient and keep trying.

Building trust at the speed of change is a journey with no destination. But every successful journey needs a map and a vehicle for making it. It is my hope that this book provides you with both. First, everyone must begin to trust themselves. Then we can learn to trust each other. Together, will find all the answers we need.

My best wishes to each of you as we begin our journey.

Edward M. Marshall, Ph.D.
The Marshall Group, Inc.
Chapel Hill, North Carolina 27514
Tmgmarshal@aol.com

Acknowledgments

As I look into the eyes of my two boys, Jonathan and Adam, I see the hope of the future, their spark of creativity, and a desire to succeed. To you, my sons, I give this work in the hopes that it may result in a different world for you and all the other children of this world. We live in a time of peril as well as great opportunity. This book is about the good in you, and how not to give into the dark side. It is about the integrity, dignity, and honor that you bring to the world and the new millennium. To you I give the belief that you can live in a world of trust if you create it.

To my wife, Elise, I wish to express my profound appreciation for your gifts of love, patience, and wisdom that you have shown me throughout these many months, and for your inspiration when at several points all seemed lost. Thank you for your belief in me and in this work.

The opportunity to make this contribution was possible only because of a very special person, Adrienne Hickey of AMACOM Books. Over the past five years, Adrienne has not only shown her consistent support for this work but also has challenged me to discover new ways to communicate these important values, frameworks, and methods so that others could hear. My respect for her standards is matched only by my appreciation for her commitment.

To Steven T. Miller, trusted friend, honored colleague, and fellow traveler, I owe the deepest debt of gratitude for giving his wisdom, his love of people, his faith in the future, and his belief in me. It was Steve who kept my feet to the fire on the central tenets of this work. It was Steve who helped me define the framework. Thank you, my friend, for it is your optimism that kept me focused.

To my clients I owe a debt of gratitude, for were it not for your diligent efforts at seeking to build trust in the workplace, none of this would have been developed. You taught me all I know. You invited me into your workplaces, trusted me with your hopes, challenged me to adapt this methodology to your realities, and struggled to discover new ways to work together. Sometimes you exceeded even your own expectations. Sometimes you failed, but learned. In all of your endeavors, however, you gave of yourselves and your conviction to take the journey.

To Niels Buessom, thank you for the many hours you gave to editing this work and helping me find new and more concise ways to express myself. To Tina Bandy Barefield, a big thank-you for the graphics support and your patience with me as we went through this writing process. And to my friend, financial manager, and colleague Lorraine Osborne, thank you for your confidence in me, that we could not only keep the business on a solid footing while doing this work, but that we should do this work at all.

Finally, to every one of you reading this book, thank you for being willing to start the journey. It is worth taking. I wish you the best.

///////////////////

Before you begin, a couple of reference notes are in order. First, throughout the book I use many case examples from actual company change experiences. Although all company names are fictitious to protect their privacy, the situations described are real. Some of the case examples are composites of situations, but have been written in a way that does not detract from the points being made.

Second, there are a number of terms of art representing proprietary products and services offered by The Marshall Group, Inc., of Chapel Hill, North Carolina. These products and services include the Collaborative Method^{sm}, the Collaborative Team Formation Process^{sm}, and the Workplace Culture Index^{sm}. These service marks have been registered with the U.S. Patent Office or are pending approval, and should reflect that fact when used by others.

PART ONE

Where We Have Been, Where We Can Go

1

///

Leading at the Speed of Change

"Speed happens when people at work truly trust each other."

///

As he talked with his senior leadership team, Warren shared his deep frustration with how MSI* was going to meet its business challenges over the next three years. There were new, lower-cost competitors nipping at their market share. The speed of new product releases had increased from twelve months to seven. This meant more pressure on MSI to achieve new efficiencies without sacrificing quality or raising costs. The introduction of new technologies in marketing, production, and quality control meant dramatic changes in the way they would need to do their work.

There were also workforce pressures. Half the employee base had been loyal to MSI for an average of twenty years. Many of them were used to their jobs and were either unwilling or unable to learn the new technologies. The other half of the workforce was younger, but more willing to learn. They were motivated by lifestyle issues and were building marketable skills for their next jobs. Loyalty to MSI was not a key concern, and yet they expected management to provide more benefits and increase par-

---

*All company names are fictitious to protect the identity of the companies involved, but the circumstances described are real.

3

ticipation in decision making. They wanted to rise quickly in the company, but were able to move on if they encountered too many barriers.

MSI's business performance was satisfactory, but not stunning. The projections showed moderate growth, but forecasts were only forecasts. Customer satisfaction remained steady at 88 percent; the company needed a breakthrough. Employee satisfaction numbers were dropping, with management consistently getting low scores on measures of trust, communications, and involvement. And even though people were working longer hours, per capita production had dropped while turnover had a slight up-tick to 23 percent annually. In addition, after ten years of change programs that included total quality, reengineering, downsizing, outsourcing, and restructuring, the workforce had come to view job security as a relic of the past. Distrust was in full bloom.

Warren and two of his key change management advisers, Trevor and Sarah, huddled after the meeting to discuss how to rebuild the trust level required for MSI to meet its growth and performance targets. They knew they needed to transform the workplace one more time, but what would it look like next? What values would be needed to drive it? What covenant between leadership and the workforce would reduce fear and increase trust? What corporate framework would enable them to balance their new business realities with the needs of their people?

Business realities for all companies continue to change at blinding speed. At the same time the prevailing approach to leading and managing a business hierarchy remains essentially the same as it was in the 1950s. How we have traditionally organized ourselves appears to be out of step with the times. Is this still a winning formula? How can we expect to meet the Knowledge Era's challenges of speed and trust with an organizational philosophy based on power that creates fear and uncertainty? For the foreseeable future:

Our most critical leadership challenge is to catch up with the speed of change by transforming the predominant approach to business from a system based on power, compliance, and transactions to one based on trust, collaboration, and relationships.

///

Put another way:

///

Our challenge is to leave behind the politics of fear, and to evolve toward what will be called a *relationship-based corporation*.

///

A relationship-based corporation is a framework for leading and managing a business that honors the fundamental needs of the individual, builds trust-based relationships, and creates a work environment that can tap into the full potential, intellectual capital, and energy of the workforce, so they are able to produce breakthrough results.

What would it take for MSI to become a relationship-based corporation, to meet its many challenges, and to build trust at the speed of change? What would success look like? For MSI or any other business organization to be successful in the future, it must first commit to a *journey of evolution*, from a culture of fear to one of trust. This is both a pragmatic and an ethical response to a market built on increasing rates of speed. To make that commitment, leadership must move beyond the belief systems of the past. Second, they would adopt a philosophy that recognizes it is people who make change happen, and that the workforce must own that change to implement it successfully. This view also recognizes that speed comes from trust-based work relationships, and that a business can achieve its full potential by leveraging those relationships.

Like a spacecraft that travels at the speed of light to reach its destination, the relationship-based corporation is the most effective vehicle for reaching sustainable competitive advantage. With this approach to leading and managing, business leaders need not compromise their integrity by focusing on speed at the expense of people. *Not only are speed and trust compatible, but also there can be no sustained speed at work without trust.* If businesses want to win in the information age, they have but one choice—to evolve.

The Choice to Evolve

In a dramatically changing marketplace, businesses need speed, quality, and lower costs to compete. New competitors and the rise of global markets have driven down the costs of manufacturing, requiring every company to seek cheaper, better, and faster ways to make higher quality products. To survive in this market, businesses must be able to make fast and accurate decisions that are in the best interests of their customers and shareholders.

To increase speed and lower costs, however, businesses have used a variety of programs—like Total Quality Management (TQM), reorganization, reengineering, outsourcing, and new technologies—with mixed results. In these efforts to become more efficient, workforces have been consolidated, right-sized, and downsized. Sometimes the efforts have worked. In other instances, the results have been lower morale, less loyalty to the company, and an increase in fear and distrust. To achieve short-term goals or sustainable competitive advantage, businesses can either continue with these programs or increase their speed by building a trust-based workplace.

To complicate the choice, our leading and managing practices have not kept pace with market demands for more speed and with workforce demands for more trust. We remain tied to the politics of power and the need to control. We still have hierarchical structures and cultures, when the way work gets done is increasingly networked and flat. We assume people know how to work collaboratively and in teams, when they do not have the understanding, skills, or incentives to do so.

The predominant approaches to business leadership and management are presently inadequate to meet the demands of the future. Top-down structures are too slow for reaching decisions. Command decisions do not involve the people who must implement them; they have little sense of ownership of the enterprise. In this culture, the workforce is less likely to feel trusted, so why would it speed up production or risk trying new strategies?

Can we change our business organizations fast enough to keep up with the demands of speed? And even if we want to change, can we do so while strengthening the bonds of trust and respect in the workplace? Can it be done quickly? And when all is said and done, what type of corporation would we end up with?

These are questions that concern many business leaders. To answer them will require a positive commitment to change the current way of working, a conscious choice to evolve the business organization to a new and higher level. In so doing, however, we will come face to face with our own self-imposed limitations and the very hard realities of real change. Change is fine until *we* have to work differently. New leadership styles and behaviors make sense until we must give something up or take a leap of faith and trust in others. Transforming the workplace culture is fine unless it costs too much time and money. So there must be a compelling enough need for the business and its leaders to change.

The Compelling Need to Change

The conscious choice to evolve a business is predicated not only on new marketplace realities but also on where we have been. Let's look briefly at two value systems that reflect the way we have successfully managed our businesses during the twentieth century: our heritage of compliance; and the rise of the transaction-based corporation. Then we'll look at three key drivers that create the compelling need to change the corporation in the twenty-first century: (1) the need to rebuild trust after years of change experiments; (2) the need for speed to meet market demands; and (3) the expectations of a changing workforce.

Models That Dominated the Twentieth Century

A Heritage of Compliance and Transactions

Hierarchy has been the cornerstone of business leadership for some time. Compliance has been its management operating system. In a hierarchical organization, everyone is "incented" to function in accordance with the rules of power, command, and control. A knowledge-based economy, however, relies on relationships that are networked and trust-based, and can produce quick responses. Today's marketplace will not give us the time to go up and down the chain of command to get a decision made. In a global economy, we must have the confidence that our teammates are competent and will do the right thing for the business. Authority is no longer the glue that holds the workforce together—trust is.

The use of power and control to get things done also does not really work in the long term. People tend to vote with their energy. They comply with what is necessary to keep their jobs, but their creativity, pride, commitment, and innovation may not be fully utilized. They walk out the door at the end of the day, and take their intellectual capital and loyalty with them.

Force does not produce superior results. It does not produce loyalty. It does not increase profits, nor does it satisfy customers in the long term. In fact, it is difficult to command anyone to do anything these days. Organizations whose *modus operandi* is the use of force or control to get things done will quickly find they cannot keep top performers, increase productivity, or maintain their competitive posture in an age of networks and relationships.

The Transaction-Based Corporation

In the second half of the twentieth century, the leadership model evolved somewhat from the compliance system to what I will call a "transaction-based" approach. In this approach to business, work is divided into a series of tasks that require people to get the input, information, or approvals they need to get the tasks done. What matters is the "transaction" and the result—that is, getting the task completed—not the community of relationships and shared interests that provide the context for getting those transactions completed effectively. Most often, transaction-based organizations are siloed, with thick walls between the basic functions, such as manufacturing, marketing, information technology, and customer service. Sometimes these companies are matrixed, with senior managers reporting to two or more people, but with power and authority still clearly understood as coming from the top.

Power and control, however, are still very much at the core of this operating system. In the workplace, people find themselves surviving by cooperating with each other. People work to influence others to their point of view. Conflicts tend to be avoided as people learn to be "nice" rather than honest. Politics remains a critical means of getting work done, as does the rumor mill. They perform a critical function in enabling people to get their tasks completed.

In a transaction-based company, a lot of time and emphasis is spent on structure, reporting relationships, and accountability systems. Communications across the silos are usually on a "need to know" basis or are tied to a specific transaction. Senior managers may or may not know what others are doing, but because their focus is internal, on their own groups, there is little if any alignment across the organization in a common business direction.

Leadership comes from the top, as in the traditional hierarchical organization, and transaction-based leaders usually need to be at the center of the information flow. They manage by politics and persuasion, but ultimately have the ability to fire their direct reports—and everyone knows it. "Compliance with a velvet glove" is how one vice-president put it.

Teams are often formed in the transaction-based corporation, but they tend to behave more like committees, are driven by a senior management agenda, are usually not facilitated, and have decisions made by majority rule or by the senior manager.

Ownership and buy-in for key decisions are not high priorities, and as a result most members of the workforce end up not knowing, and sometimes not caring, about the results. But nowhere does the cloak of cooperation disappear faster than at budget time, when the velvet gloves often come off.

Because the workforce, and often leadership, does not have the same shared view of where the company is going, getting work done is slowed down. There are missed communications and misunderstandings across departments about what needs to be done, and decisions are documented for fear that someone will hold them accountable. Distrust is the hallmark of this culture. If you're afraid to act for fear of losing your job, or if you do not have the information you need to act, or do not feel ownership in the result, it is unlikely that speed, high quality, and profit are going to be the result.

Is this kind of workplace going to enable businesses to meet the demands of a globally networked, high-speed market? If companies want to be successful in the information age, they do have a choice to evolve from this heritage of compliance and transactions to become *relationship-based*.

Key Drivers for the Twenty-First Century

There are three additional reasons business leaders might consider this journey.

Rebuilding Trust After Years of Change Experiments

The 1990s were heralded by some business experts as "the decade of relationships," when inspired leadership, people-focused management practices, and total quality work processes would result in a high-performance organization, delighted customers, and increased profitability. It was instead a decade of chaos and fear, a time when major structural changes and massive layoffs resulted in broken covenants, lost loyalty, and distrust. Families suffered, friendships were affected, and the productive energy of the workforce was damaged. There was little common ground remaining upon which to stand. And there was much confusion about what was needed next as companies continued to look for lower costs and greater efficiencies.

Businesses were not transformed during this time. Instead, workplaces became bunkers, where many tried to maintain their professionalism in the midst of the chaos. Leadership philosophies and practices ranged from Attila the Hun to Mr. Rogers. Structures were either centralized, decentralized, or both. Some organizations were flattened while others maintained a strict hierarchy. By the end of the decade, there was no clear direction. It was every company for itself, and every employee for themselves.

In all this change, we have lost a lot. With the drive to be competitive at almost any price, we lost our innocence. The psychological contract that was the legacy of the previous generation is gone. Business leadership lost some credibility as an environment of "we" and "they" emerged. Sure, there were teams, but the strategic decisions were made elsewhere. The job of the workforce was to implement efficiently and effectively. Many found themselves coping rather than buying in, compromising rather than consenting. Some people found themselves saying, "OK, I can live with that" because it seemed there were few alternatives.

We have lost a sense of control over our own destiny, and find ourselves at the mercy of forces beyond our control—speed, shareholders, new technologies, and unrelenting change. In the process, we have lost a sense of community. We now live in a virtual workspace where relationships are defined by the transactions we must complete to get a task done. We are expected to figure it out and have fruitful work relationships across vast geographic areas. We believe we must "just do it now," which may mean ignoring process; we need to get results no matter what. We come together only to get the next project finished or to meet a business objective.

But perhaps the greatest casualty may be our self-confidence. While there are exceptions, many people have lost the feeling that their opinions really matter, that they will be treated fairly and honestly. The sense of what is right and fair in work relationships seems to have given way to what is expedient; and the sense that people could change things for the better gave way to skepticism and even despair.

In spite of what we have lost, however, we can still heal the wounds of the past and put aside the distrust. But it will take awareness, a clear focus, a methodology that can be implemented, and our integrity to make sure it happens. We have an opportunity now to evolve toward a new approach to work, a new management operating system based on relationships. We can rebuild the trust that is the cornerstone of sustained competitive advantage—but it will take a new level of commitment.

The Need for Speed

///

The new senior vice-president at TransAm, a transportation company, had just finished his first meeting of the joint management-labor leadership team. In his closing remarks, he pointed to the importance of having their cooperation, and the importance of the decisions they had made in this two-day meeting. He then suggested that next month's meeting be cut in half. The following month, he had the team cut its time in half yet again. Three months out, the meetings that used to be two days in length, bringing opportunities for dialogue, problem solving, and trust building between labor and management, were now a mere two hours, run by the senior executive. There was virtually no dialogue. Decisions were getting made, but they were made before the meeting. There was no ownership, only compliance. The partnership collapsed, and everyone returned to an adversarial relationship, the victim of the need to control rationalized in the name of speed.

///

There is no debate about the need for speed. It is, rather, how we create that speed that will distinguish the winners. I recall the high school math course where we learned about cutting numbers in half, and we debated whether there really was a number called "zero." In certain aspects of business, zero may be possible, but in the workplace we often need to go slow so we can go fast.

In the last twenty years, we have again and again seen new technologies cut production or development time in half. The standard for package delivery used to be four to seven days—that is, until overnight delivery changed the way we do business. International calls used to be done through trunk lines; now we dial 011 to be hooked up by satellite instantly. We used to talk at the water cooler; now we send e-mail. We used to go to the office; now we network from airports, hotels, and home offices. Our expectations for a prompt response used to be measured by days; now it is measured in nanoseconds. The entire business agenda, including the quality of our decisions and our relationships, is defined by how fast we act.

We do not control speed, so we end up reacting to it. Speed is amorphous and yet it frames our actions. We cannot touch it, and yet it is all around us. Speed is driven by expectations others have about our response time, which then become an assumption, and then a standard or measure of performance and success. We find ourselves following a standard no one is controlling. But if we do not react to change quickly enough, we can lose the customer, the sale, our competitive position, and even our jobs.

Speed is a dictum, a measure of individual, team, and organizational competence and performance. Individuals are expected to multitask and multitrack. Teams are expected to "just do it" and not spend time planning and front-loading a project, even though the downstream costs of inadequate planning prove far more time-consuming. We focus on short-term results with little concern for the long-term impact.

In the drive for speed, however, we may lose perspective on how to best attain it. You don't get a job done quickly by doing more things faster. Speed is achieved by having trust-based relationships in which there is confidence that actions taken, even if in haste, are in our mutual self-interest. If people are aligned in a common strategic direction and trust each other's motives, then all will move faster. But time must be taken on the front end to build that trust.

The power-based organization cannot adapt fast enough to keep pace with the rate of change in the market or meet the needs of the workforce. The need for speed through trust, then, offers a compelling reason to change.

The Expectations of a Changing Workforce

The expectations of the workforce today go far beyond Maslow's hierarchy of needs, whereby economic survival requirements must be met before people can begin to innovate. If we learned anything from the experimentation of the 1990s, it was that the fundamental needs of the workforce have little to do with economics. The workforce wants to be trusted, respected, to have an opportunity to learn and grow, to contribute, to win, and to be acknowledged. They expect to be involved in decisions that affect their jobs, their teammates, and their futures. Top performers expect opportunities to grow, enhanced benefits, and a workplace where they can take risks and innovate.

Furthermore, the workforce expects leadership to walk the talk and to operate with integrity. When there is integrity in the workplace, hard work, speed, efficiency, loyalty, and profitability naturally follow. The extent to which the compliance and transaction-based approaches to management do not meet these expectations, or violate the fundamental need for integrity and trust, will determine how well those business organizations will be able to compete.

In summary, then, what is the compelling need to change the way we get work done? Neither the hierarchical form of organization nor the transaction-based corporation is capable of building the level of trust in work relationships that will enable businesses to meet the market's need for speed. New information technologies, tools, and simplified processes alone will not produce trust. Power will not create it. The relationship-based approach recognizes that people working in a trust-based workplace will respond quickly, instinctively, and without resistance. We must enable the corporation to evolve to the next stage.

The Next Stage of Corporate Evolution

What is the next stage? What if we developed an organizational system that gave people what they say they need in order to excel in these fast-paced times? What if we could transform our businesses in a way that would achieve breakthrough results without breaking the will of the workforce?

Inform, Inc., is just such a company. As a start-up high-technology company, it was founded by three partners who decided to create a business that would grow with the speed of change

by building a workplace based on trust, respect, and integrity. They decided to lead and manage collaboratively, making strategic decisions using true consensus as their rule. They built a structure that was flat, team-based, and focused on the customer. Hundreds of associates all across the country were networked, organized into customer clusters that reflected the necessary skills and competencies those customers needed. Cross-functional and cross-trained, these customer teams were flexible, service-based, and focused on quality, as well as the bottom line.

The human resources function was handled by the partners with the help of a professional adviser. The partners were cross-trained in a range of leadership methods and people processes, such as how to build ownership of the company's business and culture; how to align the workforce with the strategy; and how to develop collaborative teams. Innovation, creativity, and risk were rewarded, at both individual and team levels. Leadership was considered a function, not a position. There were no titles, not even a formal president; business problems were solved collaboratively among key players who had the skills necessary to solve them.

Impossible? Inform, Inc., has been growing at an average of 60 percent a year for the last three years, and it expects to become multinational in the next three years. Not only is it possible, but this relationship-based corporation may be a model for the future.

This new approach to work has also been taken in a few older manufacturing firms. For example, the president of Qual-Tex thought such a work environment was indeed impossible. This fifty-year-old heavy manufacturing plant had been managed by business leaders who had succeeded with the command approach to business. But with its market exploding and seeing the need to meet dramatically increased demands for speed, quality, and product diversification, the president and his top advisers realized they needed a new approach to managing their business. They searched for two years for an approach that would work, tried this program and that, brought in outside managers, and gradually formed their leadership team around the principles of collaboration and alignment. With fits and starts, they took their newfound faith in each other and their team to the rest of the business. They got rid of time clocks, created customer-focused teams across rapidly disappearing departments, and set up a two-way communications process that had line workers challenging executives on how best to get the work done. As part of a team-based organization, everyone learned new people skills, learned new technologies, and drove the accident rate down to near zero. With incentive-based pay tied to quarterly performance, there was a focus on mutual support across all three shifts.

When all was said and done, this mature business was able to reinvent itself—not through structural change or the program of the month, but by a culture-first, principle-based commitment to leading and managing their business for the good of all. They built a truly collaborative, relationship-based corporation and gave everyone in the business a stake in the future.

The Future Is Now

The future business organization will evolve not only because of a compelling need to increase speed, but also because becoming a trust-based workplace is the right thing to do for the workforce. Most of us want to move from a culture of fear to one of trust. To do that we must change our traditional organizational framework to one that values principle over power, people over process and technique, and that teaches us how to strengthen relationships and collaboration at all levels.

The organizations that embark on this journey will recognize that the solution lies within each of us and is very much our responsibility to achieve. We cannot shift the responsibility for true change to a program, a tool, or a technology; people make change happen. These organizations will understand that the journey requires a permanent commitment to change, a willingness to look in the mirror, and the capacity to realign how we do work. There will be a recognition that we get work done only through people, and that people are our only true competitive advantage.

There will also be a recognition by these companies that a

new level of maturity in business leadership is necessary to guide this evolution. Leaders will not only move out of denial that the command approach works, but also beyond the notion that the heroic leader is the answer. They will open themselves up, take risks, learn new skills, and try new approaches to achieve collaboration. They will realize that they must move beyond politics and influence, beyond gimmicks and public relations in their relationships with their workforce. They will look in the mirror and search for their authentic selves, so that they can bring not only their intellect and competency but also heart and soul to the business. This book provides the framework for this journey.

The Journey to the Relationship-Based Corporation

Speed happens when people trust each other. Building trust and developing a relationship-based corporation are the only way to achieve superior performance and sustainable competitive advantage in the future. For some companies, the question may be whether to evolve at all. For others, it will be how. We must learn new ways to do so at the speed of change, without sacrificing the trust of the workforce.

But our organizations will mature only as we ourselves mature. As one of my mentors wisely said about the phenomenon of organizational evolution, "The river is going that way. Which way are you going?" The journey will not be easy. We must evolve from the inside out—from our core values and beliefs outward to how we express them, with integrity, in our relationships, actions, and lives. The entire framework for our organizational culture, processes, and structures will change from what we know today. And we will need to withstand the rigors of the journey itself and learn new ways to avoid reverting to old habits.

To withstand these rigors, we will discover that how we begin the journey is how we will end up. To become a relationship-based corporation, we must have a change methodology that builds ownership, trust, mutual respect, and integrity. As the leadership, workforce, and organization go through the trials of self-discovery and change, they will realize that the three critical ingredients for success will be their Character, Will, and Discipline. Their Character will be reflected in the values and beliefs that result from a commitment to the journey. Their Will to honor that commitment is reflected in the ability to look in the mirror, to make the necessary changes and to put the processes and capacity in place to achieve success. Their Discipline will be reflected in their patience in the face of adversity, and persistence in the face of resistance. They will remember why the journey was begun in the first place, and will act from a deep level of integrity, stay the course, learn, and grow.

The remainder of our journey together is in two basic parts, involving eight chapters and an epilogue. In the next three chapters, we more closely examine the current state of business organization and see what the future vision could look like.

In Chapter 2, we will look at the culture of fear that defines today's dominant business model—the transaction-based corporation. We will see how the culture of fear creates a cycle of distrust and how easy it is for us to become entrapped in that cycle. We will also learn the seven steps we can take to break that cycle and begin building trust-based relationships.

In Chapter 3, we will explore why successful business organizations need to be grounded in the principle of trust. We will learn that a fundamental driver for the workforce is called the trust imperative—that is, that trust is a fundamental need people have to be able to operate at their full potential. We will look at what it means to trust ourselves, and how the degree of leadership self-trust impacts organizational performance.

In the fourth chapter, a vision of the future business organization will be described—a future that institutionalizes the trust-based workplace. A comprehensive description of the relationship-based corporation will include its approach to customers, culture, leadership, work processes, structure, systems, and outcomes. This future, the reader will realize, is feasible, but the focus must be on its successful creation.

Part Two focuses on the actual process of evolution, the implementation journey, and what it takes to succeed. Based on lessons learned in the last several decades of structural and process-based changes, we will not only describe a proven change methodology, but will also look at the specifics of how to ensure success at various levels of business.

In Chapter 5, I introduce the Collaborative Method, a means of culture-first change that has been successfully employed in a wide range of business change processes during the last decade. From the application of this approach we will discover the critical ingredients for a successful change process, including the core principles of character, will, and discipline.

Chapter 6 has been dedicated to describing the five phases involved in implementing the Collaborative Method. At each point along the way, specific tools and processes are suggested that will strengthen the probability of success.

In Chapters 7, 8, and 9, respectively, we will look at how the change principles of Character, Will, and Discipline apply to three levels of change: leadership, the workforce, and the organization as a whole. We will discover that leadership integrity; a unified, fully responsible workforce; and alignment of the organization are all fundamental to successful change. But along the way, after the specific success profile for each level is defined, we will discover the obstacles that stand in the way and the interventions and conscious choices that can be made to achieve the breakthroughs needed.

Finally, in the Epilogue, I close with some thoughts on what we have learned, and what the future can look like if we choose to balance the needs of the workforce with the requirements of speed, quality, and profit.

My bias is clear, but it is based on experience. This book rests on the conviction that we *do* have a choice in how to lead and manage our business organizations. We can continue operating in the style of the industrial age or we can meet the challenges of the Knowledge Era head-on. The relationship-based corporation works. It works because it rests on the principle of trust and the recognition that it is people who do the work and implement change. So, if we are to build trust at the speed of change, we must invite both leadership and the workforce to take this journey together.

Let's begin.

2

//

The Transaction-Based Corporation: A Culture of Fear and Distrust

"A scared man can't work."
—Frank, shop foreman for twenty-five years

//

Harrison stormed into the office to meet with a key adviser and fumed, "It makes no difference what I do around here anymore. Every time I try to do the right thing for my customer, Fred under-cuts me. He committed my right hand, Janice, to a new technology project that has a report due next Friday. She is key to our strategic planning retreat this week. I've been planning it for two months, have people from all over the country coming in, and he decides without my consultation to pull her off the team twenty-four hours before my meeting. Now I must absorb the cost, the lost time, and credibility with our customers."

With probing from his adviser, Harrison continued by paint-ing a not-too-flattering portrait of how his company operated. "Fred is the boss. I usually do whatever he tells me to because he has the bigger picture. He does have the 'right' to dip into my organization, but he ought to talk with me first. He is hard to reach, and when I do, he always has his own agenda. He tells me to come in only when I have a problem. And yet I when I do, I never leave feeling we discuss anything. Our senior leadership team does not work like a team; it is a series of one-way interactions with Fred. We don't plan or make strategic decisions. My performance is measured by profitability, not by how well I manage my division. Fred never asks how my people are doing unless it has a direct bearing on a short-term result. And then he wonders why our employee and customer satisfaction ratings are so low.''

Many companies today operate this way. Harrison's company is what we will call a transaction-based corporation. In a transaction-based company, the job gets done, but neither leadership nor the workforce may be happy about it. Resources are optimized, but often the workforce is suboptimized. Business leaders focus on structure and the bottom line, rather than on workplace morale or workforce productivity. The transaction-based approach to work dominates how we think about leading our business organizations. If we are to lead at the speed of change, it is this approach we must change.

This evolution, however, is extremely difficult to bring about. To understand that difficulty, we will first define what is meant by a "transaction-based corporation" and describe its key drivers, including the culture of fear. Second, we will look at the cycle of distrust that is created by this approach to business, and how this distrust reduces a company's ability to lead at the speed of change. Finally, we will examine what it takes to break the cycle of distrust so that the company can begin its evolution toward a relationship-based approach to work.

Defining the Transaction-Based Corporation

The values of the transaction-based corporation are not that much different from the more traditional command organization. Power and control are the core of its philosophy, but there are teams and there is a bit more workforce participation. Unlike a traditional hierarchy, however, the transaction-based corporation is more focused on the exchange of information needed to complete a given task or project. At the same time, responsibility still flows downward, while accountability still goes upward. Let's define it more specifically.

Webster defines *transaction* as a "communicative action or activity involving two parties or things that reciprocally affect or influence each other." To put this in a business context:

//

A transaction-based corporation is a system whose leadership, workforce, culture, structure, and processes are driven by the authority of the transaction, the task, or the result, as well as the leader.

//

In a transaction-based organization, power resides at the top; the workforce is focused on the exchange of information and the completion of tasks or projects, not necessarily on the quality, character, or impact of those tasks on work relationships. It is an organization that cares more about individual performance than that of groups or teams. It is dedicated primarily to output and shareholder value. The people side of the business, such as teamwork and skills development, are usually viewed as a means to an end.

To help you better understand the transaction-based approach to work, what follows are ten elements of this framework. Figure 2-1 provides a summary of these elements, which are then described in more detail.

• *The value system*. Three core values drive the transaction-based business: cooperation, power, and efficiency. First is the value of cooperation. People work together cooperatively in the sense that their transactions are based on some level of shared commitment to a common goal, supported by economic incentives and benefits that shape motivation and commitment. Harrison and Fred will be nice to each other as long as their own needs get met. The authority structure requires them to do so, and their performance-based incentives provide the financial incentive to back it up. People will be nice to each other as long as their own needs get met, otherwise politics, influence, trade-offs, and negotiations will be used to achieve the objectives of their business units.

The second core value is that of power and control, which are central to the functioning of the transaction-based company. Power is vested in the top leadership, as well as in the importance of the transactions required to achieve strategic objectives. Informal power and influence become critical because the way to get things done involves a constant process of positioning, doing favors, keeping your head down, making yourself indispensable, negotiating, and building alliances that will ensure

Figure 2-1. The transaction-based system.

VALUE SYSTEM	Cooperation; power and control; efficiency
RESULTS ORIENTATION	Optimize; short-term focus
STRATEGIC DIRECTION	Top down; alignment at the top of the organization
LEADERSHIP	Top down but engaged; does not delegate decisions; everyone knows who is the boss
CUSTOMER-VENDOR CHAIN	They matter, but are not partners; take orders -- give orders; do not focus on shared planning or problem-solving
PSYCHOLOGICAL CONTRACT WITH WORKFORCE	Contract is temporal, based on skills; no job security
ORGANIZATIONAL STRUCTURE	A siloed organization; teams at the top; change created through restructuring; competition a value
WORKPLACE CULTURE	Nice but not honest; people are fearful; avoid conflict
HOW WORK GETS DONE	Majority rule; boss breaks tie; by transactions of information; some teams, but not team-based; manage upward as well as cross-functionally
PRODUCTIVE CAPACITY	The organization is able to tap into only a small percentage of the productive energy of the workforce

your success. But when the chips are down or earnings are disappointing, management usually does not hesitate to assert the control necessary to drive the business forward.

The third core value is that of efficiency in business processes, where the focus is on the optimal use of scarce resources. Structures will be changed, new technologies introduced, and new processes put in place to increase efficiencies. Typically, little emphasis is placed on tapping into the intellectual capital or hidden productivity of the workforce. In fact, in this model, labor is considered a cost. When they are financially stressed, transaction-based companies usually opt to reduce headcount without taking into full consideration the impact the reduction will have on workforce morale or efficiency.

• *Results orientation.* At the end of the day, the transaction-based corporation is focused on increasing shareholder value, customer satisfaction, and profitability, even if that means there must be some sacrifice on the human side of the enterprise. The workforce must adopt this focus on short-term results or move on. There is an impatience with process, front-loaded planning, and building ownership in the workforce. There is a bias for action, even if it may be in the wrong direction.

• *Strategic direction.* The strategic direction of a transaction-based corporation is usually based on leadership's view of the market and the processes they believe are necessary to realize the company's objectives. Sometimes this direction is tied to what customers need, but more likely it is linked to increasing the company's market share or profitability. This approach usually does not involve the rest of the organization. Rollouts for high participation in the creation of the company vision do not happen. Instead, the vision, mission, strategic objectives, and performance expectations are communicated to the workforce. Sometimes there are feedback sessions, but without meaningful involvement of the workforce, alignment is not possible. This can lead to the business's moving off in a direction that may be out of step with the market, internal core values, and/or the capabilities of the workforce.

A transaction-based approach to strategic positioning may

also leave the business vulnerable, unable to leverage workforce loyalty, commitment, or wisdom about the market. Often, strategic moves such as joint ventures, alliances, mergers, or acquisitions are initiated without the benefit of this wisdom. The high failure rate of these moves attests to the importance of such alignment.

• *Leadership.* The fainthearted need not apply for top leadership positions in a transaction-based corporation. Strong egos and even charismatic personalities are essential for successful senior leadership. At the same time, second- and third-level managers must be able to subordinate their own egos to those of their leaders. This typically means that the primary job of middle managers is to manage upward. Peer relationships are not the primary concern, though they are still important.

For a transaction-based leadership team, the focus is usually on status updates. Decisions are made elsewhere. Leadership may seek advice, but it tends not to delegate decision-making responsibility to the team. As one senior business leader put it, "Sure we can have a meeting without Warren, but there is no point. If he's not behind it, it won't happen."

Communications are transacted both in and outside of the meetings among individual leaders. Problems are solved one-on-one. One's ability to get resources and resolution to key business issues depends on the individual's influence with that manager. Priorities come from the top rather than the bottom. You can be preempted at any time.

Like Fred, transaction-based business leaders are usually not deterred from their course of action, or approach, by statistics about problems or dysfunctions in the workplace that might show up on employee satisfaction surveys. Even though many managers believe that most business issues stem from people problems, such as interpersonal conflicts and failures to communicate effectively, they tend to simply push harder for a strategic, technical, or programmatic solution to their business issues. The maxim for this type of leader is: "If it becomes necessary, I'll not hesitate to make the decision."

• *The customer-vendor chain.* In a transaction-based company, the customers matter, but mostly as interactions involving the taking and filling of orders in a timely manner. Vendors also matter to the extent that they can meet the company's time, cost, and quality requirements. The company sets the parameters and gives the orders, and the vendor either meets them or does not. Here is the distinction that needs to be made: In a company that values relationships, in addition to the actual transaction, there is more emphasis on seeing the vendor-company-customer linkage as a chain of relationships, each of which is critical to the success of the other. When a critical decision or problem arises, rather than terminating the business relationship, the parties sit down to work it through. The value of the relationship is measured by more than just dollars or quantitative statistics in the short term; it is measured by the character and integrity of company-to-company relationships over time.

• *The psychological contract with the workforce.* In a transaction-based company, little attention is given to the notion of a "psychological contract"—that is, the exchange of services and loyalty for job security and satisfaction. In the transaction-based corporation, the fundamental assumption driving the contract is a calculus of the individual's value versus their cost to the company. The individual's value is measured by their willingness and capacity to grow or learn new techniques. In a transaction-based company, individuals work for a wage and for personal advancement. Loyalty is valued to a certain extent, but is not always a critical factor in key management decisions. For the individual worker, then, value and meaning in work are found in the social groups and informal ties they develop on their own.

• *Organizational structure.* The mental model of the transaction-based corporation, shown in Figure 2-2, is a stovepiped or siloed organization. This organizational structure has not evolved much from the hierarchical model. Authority is still top-down, but with some teams included. The work of middle management and the front line, however, is done by department, with some informal cooperation across departmental lines. People work within their silos and report upward. Sometimes they are actively discouraged from communicating across silos, even if necessary to get the work done. Competition is valued, and sometimes groups are pitted against each other to increase output. Change occurs by restructuring work relationships-centralizing, decentralizing, downsizing, or outsourcing.

• *The workplace culture.* Nowhere in the transaction-based corporation is the reality of power and exchange-based work clearer than in the workplace culture. Behind all the slogans for participation, teams, total quality, and empowerment lies the real driver of human behavior: fear. At one end of the spectrum, there is the fear of job loss, being written up, or retribution. But far more powerful for some employees is the fear of not measuring up to the expectations of supervisors, not being considered a top performer, or—worse yet—being embarrassed in one's peer group by being excluded from projects or processes that matter.

Figure 2-2. The transaction-based structure.

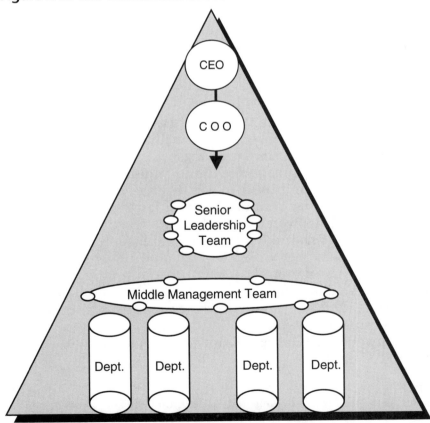

The operating premise for working in a fear-based culture is to be "nice, but not honest." Candor is not rewarded. Conflicts are avoided or dealt with off-line. The rumor mill provides a way for people to share their truths or perceptions about how the organization really works. This culture is not always obvious to the outside observer, however. Sometimes it is denied, but people will comply and cooperate because it is a lot easier to do so. After all, the culture may not be so bad that it is worth losing a job over; besides, there are few companies that are any different.

- *How work gets done.* Work does get done, but usually with some difficulty. Sometimes, work gets done in spite of the realities of the workplace. Information is exchanged to complete tasks or projects. Decisions are made at the upper levels of the business. If problems are not solved where they happen, they are sent up the line.

In terms of group conduct, there may be some teams, but they operate more like committees, with a power-based leader, a task, and a deadline. Team decisions are usually driven by the 80–20 principle, majority rule, or "can live with" compromises that members make to get along. Reaching a 100 percent consensus is considered too cumbersome and inefficient.

- *Productive capacity.* In a fear-based workplace, the productive capacity of the workforce usually is fairly low. Without knowing where the business is going, being afraid to make a mistake, and not being involved in the decision-making process, the workforce has little reason to go the extra mile. Creativity is often stifled. Survey results have confirmed this observation.[*] When respondents were asked what they felt their productivity capacity was, they said it was only a fraction of their potential. When asked why they were less productive than they wanted to be, respondents uniformly pointed to the fear in their workplaces as the chief culprit. Because they did not feel respected or trusted, there was a drop in their commitment, energy, and enthusiasm for the work.

Why does this happen? Remember Harrison? Now, let's listen to Felicia.

---

[*]During 1985–1999, more than 25,000 people in one hundred companies were assessed by The Marshall Group, Inc., to determine the key factors responsible for their productive capacity.

//

The Cycle of Distrust

"I can't go in to see him," Felicia said. "Every time I try to tell him how I feel, I end up listening for an hour to how wonderful it is here at First Financial, and how lucky I am. If I disagree with him, he cuts me off, gets red in the face, and raises so many objections to my point of view that I end up having to go along with him just to get out of his office. I just don't trust him anymore to treat me with respect."

Over lunch Felicia's friends were coaching her on how to deal with Martin, who admittedly was quite strong-willed. What was she afraid of? They knew. They had experienced his rage in private and his sarcasm in public. Martin never admitted to these concerns. In fact, he had quite a different view of himself—as an enlightened manager trying to empower his people but hold them accountable. Their advice to her was to steer clear and stay focused on the job. The cycle of distrust continued. How does this happen?

//

The Six Steps of the Cycle

The root cause of distrust is fear. At First Financial, the workforce was fearful. The transaction-based philosophy was deeply rooted in their culture. It was unlikely to change. Sensitivity training was not going to change Martin's attitude; he had been operating this way for twenty years. But more than just a fearful transaction was at work here. Behind this situation was a far deeper concern—what we call the *cycle of distrust*. As Figure 2-3 suggests, fear and distrust do not just happen. They are part of each of us. They feed on each other. More profoundly, they are part of the ethos of our companies, of leadership philosophies, and are ingrained in how we work with each other.

The cycle of distrust goes beyond the walls of a company. It is part of the values we have, the behaviors we exhibit, and the choices we make at work. This cycle is at the heart of our organi-

Figure 2-3. The cycle of distrust.

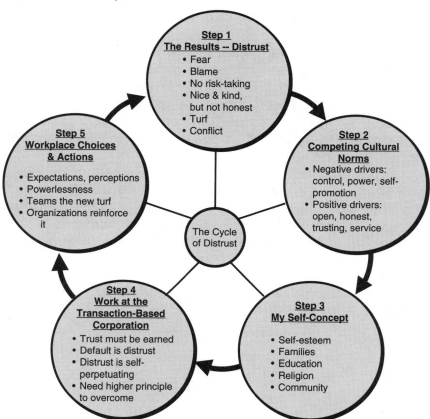

zational pain and our inability to transform our businesses. The cycle may seems impossible to break, but it is part of a work landscape we have learned to tolerate. Yet we can and must break this cycle if we are ever going to build trust at the speed of change.

How does it work?

Step 1. The Results—Distrust

We start with the end of the cycle, for the toll of institutionalized distrust is enormous—on individuals, teams, the whole workforce, and customers.

///

At Stanform Chemical, Jerry, a maintenance foreman, had made the mistake of not closing a sludge valve when he went off duty one morning at 5:00. The result was a huge fish kill, very negative media coverage, and a black eye for the company's environmental reputation. He was immediately suspended. After a competence and safety hearing, Jerry was placed on probation for three years, but only after some of his teammates testified in his favor. They pointed to the fact that Jerry had been working double shifts for three weeks to pay for increased medical bills that had resulted from his mother's heart attack. They also pointed out that there were no internal audit controls, family leave policies, or emergency financial relief programs at Stanform that could have helped Jerry. His choices were either to work extra hours or drain his savings and sell his home. Apparently management found that it was easier to blame the person than to understand and solve the problem. Jerry never trusted his management again—only his team.

///

The results of the cycle of distrust are significant. How can you trust anyone when the emphasis is on escaping blame? How can you take risks to increase productivity when the culture rewards not getting caught making mistakes? These workplaces are also characterized by internal competition and conflict rather than a unified focus on external competitors. Of the thousands of business leaders I have surveyed in the last twenty years, most say they spend more than 60 percent of their time dealing with turf battles, egos, politics, and trying to reach incentive compensation goals. This leaves only 40 percent of their time to address the needs of the customer, to develop strategy, or to improve business operations.

We seem to have created corporate cultures that value conflict avoidance over conflict resolution, and that promote behavior that is nice, but not honest. In a transaction-based workplace, it is more important to be right than to be in a relationship. No one deliberately set out one day to create work cultures that would foster an environment of distrust and fear. But unless we choose otherwise, that is our destiny.

Step 2. Competing Cultural Norms

Felicia had a choice. On the one hand, she felt a need to act in terms of her self-preservation and job security, so she did not confront Martin with her concerns. On the other hand, she wanted to be able to tell the truth, to work through her differences with him. Without a workplace culture that would support that approach, she was left with the rumor mill to say how she really felt. Felicia, Martin, and the company all lost.

Like Felicia and Martin, our beliefs, behaviors, and actions are influenced by a complex set of powerful drivers or norms. For example, one set of drivers focus on the need for control, power, and self-promotion. They focus on the "I"—what *I* need for job security, for control, and to feel good about myself. My focus, then, is on upward mobility, sharing only that information needed to support *my* goals and building the alliances *I* need to success. *I* need to be right, and will work overtime to ensure that *I* am noticed and not embarrassed. When this set of drivers is the primary set of values in the workplace, the emphasis is on transactions, politics, and power.

Another set of drivers or norms speak to the desire to be open, honest, trusting, and to serve others. These drivers focus on the "We" in an organization—the group, the team, the well-being of the company, and the needs of the customer. In this approach to work, the focus is on working through differences, taking responsibility, sharing information, and serving others. If this approach becomes the way the culture works, there is an increased possibility for trust, flexibility, and change.

Our choices, actions, and behaviors may be the result of both sets of drivers. How we determine which norms are more important than others at any given point determines whether or not we create trust in our work relationships.

Step 3. My Self-Concept

How Harrison, Fred, Felicia, Martin, or any one of us copes with the hard realities of everyday work life is shaped in great part by how we feel about ourselves. Do we have high, medium, or low self-esteem? How confident are we? How were we trained to deal with conflict in our families? Were our families functional or dysfunctional? How did our experiences affect our ability to cope with stress, moral challenges, or multiple pressures?

Entire libraries have been written on the psychological, social, and theological foundations of human behavior. It is certainly not the purpose here to attempt that type of analysis. The point is to understand that the cycle of distrust starts and ends with us, as governed by the multiple influences that shaped our self-concept: our cultural norms as interpreted by our families; how we were treated by our parents and siblings; our educational background; our community and social relationships.

When Jerry was asked why he took the actions he did, putting himself at risk, he pointed to his grandfather's advice about the value of hard work and the need to take care of one's family. Those were his drivers. Felicia learned to challenge authority as best she could. She had a difficult upbringing where direct confrontation resulted in serious punishment. We each behave in ways that are understandable based on our upbringing. For example, the drive for power or control may be compensation for a deep sense of insecurity or a childhood that felt out of control. There are many reasons why people do what they do, and it is very risky to assume that we ever know why. At the same time, it is critical that we understand the profound impact that these drivers have on the choices people make at work.

Our self-concept is also shaped by how we were taught. Many of us were taught to compete to win, to achieve, to be nice, to respect authority, to not ask the wrong questions, and to avoid embarrassment. We may have learned that power is the key to success, that who you know is often more important than what you know, or that politics may be more important than competence. We may have also learned that going along may be more conducive to long-term success than standing your ground on principle. If a workplace operates by these standards, trust can be very elusive. For us to win, others must lose. For us to be right, others must be wrong. To win, it is much easier to shift the responsibility to someone else than to own up to the consequences of our actions.

The fear of failure may drive our distrust of one another:

"At least I can count on myself." So we spend a lot of time focused on achievement, building a resume of success and forging relationships that will help us succeed or reinforce our self-concept and help promote our success. Another root of distrust may be self-doubt—a nagging belief that we may not be as successful as we think we are. Maybe we do not trust ourselves. But if we do not trust ourselves and are focused on being right, how can we possibly build trust-based relationships with others? Still another root cause may be that we were never taught how to trust others. Where would we have learned trust and collaboration? In a society preoccupied with winners and losers, superiors and subordinates, and power and control, trust is not a value we learn, even though it is the quality for which most of us want to be known. Cooperation and control are the important things to understand. In light of these root causes, we should not be surprised to find ourselves caught in the cycle of distrust.

Step 4. Work at the Transaction-Based Corporation

We all bring our own needs to work every day, and in the workplace culture just described, we try very hard to add value. It is difficult, however, given the fear we may feel, the internal competition and politics. But beneath the daily transactions, there is a far more pervasive set of forces that govern the workplace—what I call the *laws of distrust*. These laws help shape our behavior, choices, and actions, and they should help us understand how people handle change.

- *Trust must be earned; once lost, you rarely get it back.* From day one on a job, we work to build enough trust credits to establish credibility so we can get the job done. Whatever informal rules exist in the workplace dictate where the line is drawn, that, if crossed, constitutes a loss of trust. The line may be crossed without one's ever knowing it.
- *The default position is distrust.* Many people start their work relationships from the premise of distrust. Even when people work overtime to build what they believe is a high level of trust, one mistake may quickly wipe out those gains.

- *Distrust is self-perpetuating.* Distrust feeds on itself. Distrust, many people believe, will always be with us. Many feel powerless to do anything about it, which limits their ability to break the cycle.

- *Only a principle of greater power can overcome distrust.* Distrust and fear are so powerful a presence in people's work lives that only a principle of greater significance can overcome them. Trust is such a principle. But to dislodge fear and distrust, people must make a conscious choice to break the cycle.

Step 5. Workplace Choices and Actions

It is individuals, not teams or organizations, who make choices that result in trust or distrust, although choices by teams and organizations do contribute to whether the laws of distrust prevail. For most of us, our expectations, hopes, assumptions, and goals frame our choices and actions. They result in opinions being formed, conclusions being drawn, and attitudes being held. For example, Felicia assumed that Martin would be angry with her. She based that conclusion on her history and that of others. She expected his rage and acted accordingly. The result was more distrust.

Most people believe their choices at work are limited. They *are* limited if they feel victimized by others or powerless to do anything about their situation. They are also limited if they operate from their own assumptions and expectations, rather than from the possibility that things could be different. What if Felicia had approached Martin from another point of view? What if she tried to understand his pressures, asked why he reacted the way he did, and listened for understanding? What if Martin helped create a new common ground? Perhaps one of the most difficult barriers to overcome in dislodging the laws of distrust is the individual's own perceived sense of powerlessness—that there is no choice and that one person cannot really make a difference unless she is in a position of power.

Like individuals, teams can also feel a deep sense of powerlessness. Martin, for example, had a bad habit of creating teams to help him solve certain problems, but if he did not like the answer they came up with, he made the team keep working until they got the answer he wanted. The team members felt powerless to do much about the situation. They learned to find out what Martin wanted first, and then gave it to him. But they did not feel trusted to do the right thing for the company. Thus, the choices teams make will reflect the rules by which they live. Actions may be taken to overcome the sense of distrust they feel, or they may actually increase the level of conflict and fear in the organization. Teams can become either agents of change or they can become the new turf, with team charters and sponsors the new weapons to protect them.

Transaction-based organizations may also reinforce the cycle of distrust. Bureaucratic processes, accountability systems, and political pressures all play a critical role in determining the overall course of the organization and act to ensure that the boundaries are maintained. When the organization is challenged to change, more often than not its autoimmune systems of power and control kick in. The question for the evolving corporation, then, is whether management has the will to break the cycle.

Breaking the Cycle of Distrust

Tony and Gary had not spoken to one another in a civil tone for almost three years. And yet they had to work side-by-side on nearly every project. Their offices were next to each other. Their team members depended on their input. Their anger at each other was palpable, and often came out in memos or side comments to others. Their customers in the plant had found ways around their conflict to get their needs met, but it would have been a lot easier if these two had resolved their issues directly. Don, their supervisor, was on the verge of firing them both, but with three major projects coming on line at the same time, all of which required their technical skills, the pair was considered too essential to lose. With each new outburst, however, plant management's demands for a resolution increased. Time was growing short.

Don had tried everything he knew. He told the two to work it out. He listened to them individually. He sent them to the human resources department. He sent them to training. He finally decided to use outside mediation to resolve the dispute. Within four meetings, Gary and Tony had signed a partnering agreement that spelled out the rules for their new working relationship. In fact, in subsequent meetings with their teammates, they both proclaimed that the other was one of the few people at work they could trust.

The process for breaking their cycle of distrust was key. Individual interviews revealed that neither really understood the origins of the conflict, but each had a perception that had become his position toward the other. Each had plenty of supporting evidence. But both men had reached the point where they wanted the conflict to end. The pain was simply too great. It wasn't just the fear of being fired that motivated them; there was also their real desire to be at peace with themselves, each other, and their customers.

Five critical factors were responsible for their breakthrough. First, they wanted to change the situation and were given the opportunity to do so. Second, they had the strength of character to work through the process. Third, they went face-to-face to deal with their differences. Fourth, they learned that their real differences concerned style, role confusion, and communications breakdowns. Finally, they found they shared the same intent for the success of their customers. In other words, they learned through painful discovery that they had a common ground and could trust each other.

Threatening termination will not end such conflicts. Nor will insisting on cooperation; in fact, it will usually make matters worse. To break the cycle of distrust, there must be a force far more powerful than either the individuals involved or the conflict. It must be something that unites them while preserving individual integrity, and something that allows them to act together while leveraging their individual strengths. It must inspire them to do the right thing without feeling they have lost face. There needs to be an ideal to which they can aspire, a quality in each of them that can be summoned up. Trust is that principle and the common ground.

Even with trust as the standard, a successful quest to break the cycle of distrust requires the proper mind-set, training, tools, and perspective if there is to be success. People must learn how to operate at a different level. Let's look at an approach.

The Seven Steps to Breaking the Cycle

Most people may not realize they are victims of the cycle of distrust. In fact, when most people become conscious about how it works, they feel powerless to do much about it. Most people have bought into the notion that the situation is out of their control. Therefore, a *pre-condition* for even attempting to break the cycle is that the costs of distrust and fear are so high, the parties involved are prepared to abandon their points of view in order to discover a new way of working. With this realization, a phenomenal breakthrough can result and healing can occur. As Figure 2-4 suggests, there are seven essential steps to breaking the cycle of distrust.

Step 1. From Denial to Acceptance

Tony and Gary had to get out of denial about the cost of their conflict to others before the cycle could be broken. They did not realize how much everyone else on the plant site knew about their feud. They did not know that their customers consistently found ways to get things done by going around them. Don had to be willing to recognize that he could not fix it himself. Unfortunately the costs in lost time and customer dissatisfaction had to become a significant amount before they looked for another way out.

Moving from denial to acceptance usually begins with a crisis: a loss of confidence or credibility, a serious conflict in a relationship, 360-degree negative feedback, the loss of a customer, a project failure, or poor financial performance. Usually a signifi-

Figure 2-4. Breaking the cycle of distrust.

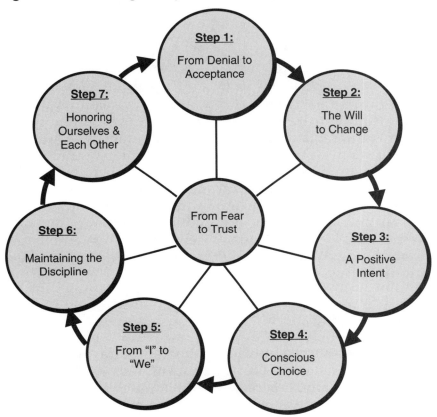

cant event either at work or at home provides the wake-up call. The people involved realize that the status quo will no longer suffice.

Even with a serious crisis on hand, individuals may still be unwilling to admit their own responsibility. To achieve full awareness of the severity of the situation, there often must be a third party who can be objective about the data, people or events. This person's job is to state the facts, help the individuals see the truth about the situation, and realize that something must change. Sometimes this process may take months or multiple events before full acceptance is achieved.

Step 2. The Will to Change

Having the will to change takes the challenge of breaking the cycle of distrust to a new level. Tony and Gary had to have the courage to come to the meetings, participate actively in the process, and arrive at new understandings about themselves and each other. To have the will to change, you need to believe in yourself and have confidence in the process of healing.

At the same time people are working diligently to break the cycle of distrust, many other factors are working against them: ego, pride, anger, perceived unfairness or disrespect, power, fear, and control. *The will to change* means recognizing these forces when they appear and moving on with the process. Breaking the cycle of distrust is not about breaking anyone down. Instead it means breaking through one's self-imposed limitations and point of view. We can only do this on a consistent basis, however, if we have a positive intent.

Step 3. A Positive Intent

Felicia had convinced herself that Martin would not listen. He ended up not listening. Gary had convinced himself that Tony was out to get him. It became a self-fulfilling prophecy. In fact, we tend to go in the direction of our most dominant thought or intent. If Felicia's intent had been to work through the issues, there might have been a different outcome. How we choose to act and behave ends up being a function of our intent. If we are clear about our intent, and it is aimed at a positive outcome, we will have a greater chance at successful relationships. Positive intent moves us from being victims of distrust to creating trust.

In organizations, if we hold the view that people are fundamentally selfish, are interested only in power or wealth, and will change only if compelled, that view will be reflected in how we act and will predispose us to the implausibility of real change. If, on the other hand, we hold the view that most people are inherently good and want to contribute, then we are more likely to believe in the possibility of change, trust, and the potential for healing.

For Tony and Gary, the cycle of distrust began to break down when they each accepted the view that the other only wanted the best for the customers. The cycle of distrust can be broken only if people have a positive intent. It reflects our faith in human nature, the acceptance of human failings, and a capacity for forgiveness. With this acceptance, a will to change, and a positive intent, we can choose to break the cycle of distrust.

Step 4. A Conscious Choice

The choice for Tony and Gary seemed so obvious. It was either resolve the conflict or be fired. But as the mediation unfolded, it was really a choice between being right or being in a good working relationship. Tony could continue to feel Gary was wrong about his approach to project management, and Gary could continue to be hurt by Tony's sarcasm. Or they could decide to have a different type of relationship.

The freedom to choose a different course of action is something we give ourselves. Usually the pain or consequences of not choosing helps us clarify the options. But even then, unless we freely choose to move through the pain of breaking the cycle, it will merely come back to us like a boomerang.

To break the cycle, people must see the opportunity and make the choice. It is rarely if ever given to us. The moment of the breakdown is probably the most difficult time to make this choice, but once that moment passes, the opportunity may never reappear. Once that conscious choice is made, however, there is a new freedom, a new level of trust. And with that trust comes the energy to create a new way of working. Without the conscious choice, the cycle cannot be broken.

Step 5. From "I" to "We"

The irony in breaking the cycle of distrust is that the focus of behavior shifts from all the attention on "I"—my concerns, my department, my issues, or my need—to "We"—how we will work together. "I" is the language of distrust, of power and control, and of organizational systems that focus on a heroic leader or the charismatic personality. "We" is the language of collaboration, team unity, and honoring leadership based on principle.

With their realization of a shared intent to serve their customers, Tony and Gary redefined their roles, developed new agreements for their work together, and became partners. This shift is almost magical when it happens, but it clearly comes from one's own volition—that is, the active choice one makes to have a working relationship based on trust.

Step 6. Maintaining the Discipline

It would have been far too easy for Gary and Tony to sign their agreement, be nice to each other, and then, when the next big issue arose, revert to their former points of view—that the other really did not mean what he said. There is always goodwill in the early stages of the trust-building process, but breaking the cycle of distrust requires intensive, ongoing work. As in a marriage that has experienced a breakdown, working your way back to trust and credibility takes time, patience, and persistence.

Most importantly, the new trust must be practiced. Like becoming a champion marathon runner, trust requires disciplined practice. Every day, every week, and sometimes every hour, the emerging trust must be strengthened and reinforced. When new breakdowns occur, the positive intent must be reclarified, choices made once again, and agreements reaffirmed.

Step 7. Honoring Ourselves and Each Other

There is no turning back. Of course, we can always succumb to our defensiveness, ego, and pride and revert to the "correctness" of our positions. That's easy. The real test of character—whether for an individual, team, or organization—is to break the cycle of distrust for good. It is to honor ourselves by behaving with integrity, keeping our word, and maturing. It is to honor each other by passionately working to create a workplace where all talents, skills, and energies can be leveraged.

In Closing

Harrison felt like a victim, undercut by Fred at every turn. Felicia felt she would never be heard by an angry Martin. Gary and

Tony were unable to resolve their feud on their own. We have all grown up in organizations where we felt out of control. These organizations, we have learned, are transaction-based, governed by power, control, and fear. In these workplaces, we learned to maintain our position by any means. But we have also learned that transaction-based corporations have another agenda. They are driven by the bottom line, focus on the short term, and see the workforce as a cost, or even a liability.

We all get caught up in the cycle of distrust that is fostered by this transaction-based culture. The fear we feel may be aggravated by personal circumstances, but it is a powerful driver nonetheless. And to break the cycle of distrust, which is created by that fear, takes Character, Will, and Discipline. After all, what if Harrison and Fred could have worked out their differences? What if Felicia could have been truly heard by Martin? What if Gary and Tony had learned the skills to work through their differences on their own? What if we created a workplace where we systematically got rid of fear and addressed the patterns of distrust so that people could take risks and realize their full potential?

It is possible. But first we must understand the principle of trust, and then see how it can be institutionalized in a relationship-based corporation.

3

///

Trust as the Common Ground

"Without trust, our relationships are merely transactions."

///

"Trust me!" Alec exclaimed, "this deal is a winner." Alec was sitting in his hotel room in Buenos Aires, conducting a teleconferenced meeting across three time zones with the project review team, whose members were in Tokyo and New York. As a new member of Antac Inc.'s senior leadership group, this was the deal of his career. It had taken six months to get the proposal to the team, and now it was time to act. But among the other team members, there were some doubts about the need to move so fast. Alec's ambitions were well known to his colleagues. Publicly people said he was a rising star. Privately some questioned his motives. They saw him cut corners too often to get ahead. His drivers seemed to be more of the "I" variety than for the good of the company.

To complicate matters, Alec had not allowed enough time for the team members to review the final pro formas. There was a deadline to meet if they were to bid on this multimillion-dollar project that some said Antac's president had been wanting for years. There was no question in Alec's mind that the deal would reap rewards for the company, but he sensed that his colleagues were skeptical. As the meeting wore on, the team raised a num-

ber of questions about the validity of the numbers, the due dili-
gence process, and whether this project could be effectively
managed at a distance. After several hours of wrangling, they
agreed to the bid despite their concerns. Unbeknownst to Alec,
however, their chief competitor had already been awarded the
contract that morning. He was too late.

//

This did not have to happen. Distrust was at work here, not the
details or the speed of the deal. This project would have meant
a lot to Antac's growth plans. But Alec's approach had backfired.
Why did he wait until the last minute to review the bid? Was
there some other agenda? Why was he pushing so hard? Did he
have a side agreement with the president? The team was looking
for answers. All Alec had wanted was for his teammates to trust
his judgment. Now that was certainly not going to happen.

Transaction-based companies, like Antac, have a hard
enough time already maintaining their competitive position in
the market without having to worry about the motives of their
managers. Increasing trust levels is usually not high on the
agenda, even though, as in Alec's case, distrust often gets in the
way. Alec had no side deals. He was merely trying to prove himself worthy of his new position on the team; but he got caught
by his assumptions about how to manipulate the review process
to get the bid approved, and a work culture where distrust was
the order of the day.

The need for speed, however, is requiring companies to
work differently. They know that time is of the essence. They
know they have to make faster and higher-quality decisions.
There is no longer any time to go up the chain-of-command for
a decision. And customers will not wait for a company to overcome its internal trust issues—they will go elsewhere. Most
companies also know that the rate of market change is only increasing. They need to respond quickly and to tap into the creative energies of their workforce so they can maintain their
competitive edge. How can they do this?

It makes sense that if we can trust the judgment of our
teammates to do the right thing, even if halfway around the

world, we will be able to increase the speed of our decision making. If there had been even a moderate level of trust between Alec and the project team, the teleconference would not have been needed, the bid would have been in on time, and Antac would have had a better chance at beating the competition. But what is this thing called trust? Where does it come from? And what does it have to do with how we lead and manage? How will it increase our speed?

Trust is the fundamental building block of human relationships. It is at the root of how we treat each other. It is a principle that governs how we perceive ourselves and how others see us. It is a standard for how we lead and manage our businesses. But can we really trust each other? Are we trustworthy? And if we cannot trust ourselves, how can we possibly trust others?

There is a paradox about trust. On the one hand, to be quick and productive we need to be trusted and need to trust those with whom we work. On the other hand, few of us were taught how to trust others. At school, in sports, and at work, we have been taught to compete to win. And in a transaction-based workplace, we may have even learned to distrust the motives of others as well as to protect ourselves.

So, how do we evolve into a workplace where high levels of trust can be achieved and sustained? How do we find that common ground that will enable us to believe in each other, trust each other's motives, and build strong relationships? It is a quest, a journey that may never end, but it is one that we need to take if we are ever going to realize the full potential of our businesses and lead at the speed of change. By taking this first step on the journey, we will lay the cornerstone for creating a relationship-based workplace.

The Quest for Trust

We start this journey with a proviso. Some people believe that trust is something that happens as the result of training, leadership development, or a technique of some kind. Experience, however, tells us that trust is a principle or an inherent quality in the character of individuals, teams, and the workplace. It is shown in how people treat others, in how they conduct their work, and in how businesses treat their customers. Regarding trust as merely a program or a technique shifts the focus away from the more fundamental questions about how organizations can evolve into trust-based workplaces.

This journey, then, is about these more fundamental questions. It is about discovering that the trust we need to be successful is already there—in us, in our teams, and in the workplace. It exists in the hopes of each individual as he comes to work each day. It is in the teams who try to solve difficult problems and work through their differences. It is in the challenges organizations face as they work to create workplaces that can meet the demands of the marketplace. The journey to a relationship-based workplace is about revealing the trust that already exists in the workplace, encouraging it to emerge, and then nurturing it so it will flourish.

In this chapter, we will look at four key elements of this important cornerstone. First, I will define *trust* in a way that will give us a common framework. Second, I will describe what I will call the trust imperative—that is, the drivers that make this principle critical to the workplace. Then I will define the values that are the foundation of trust; and finally, I show how trust levels in leadership impact business performance. This discussion sets the stage for Chapter 4, where we will define the Relationship-Based Corporation, and later chapters, which will focus on how to implement it.

A Definition of Trust

Webster has defined "trust" in the following way:

- Assured reliance on the character, ability, strength, or truth of someone or something
- One in whom confidence is placed
- A charge or duty imposed in faith or confidence, or as a condition of some relationship
- Something committed or entrusted to one, to be used or cared for in the interest of another

To trust another reflects our confidence in their character, our faith in their capacities, our reliance or even dependence on their taking care of something that is important to us. And yet our trust is usually conditional. It is not given lightly. It is at the heart of our relationships. To trust someone is a reflection of their integrity and our confidence in them. To be trusted by others means we have credibility with them. To be trustworthy means we have confidence in ourselves, and that we can count on ourselves to do what we say we are going to do.

Trust needs to be thought of in at least three ways. First, it is a principle, a cornerstone of how we choose to live our lives, and a standard we use to evaluate our own actions, as well as those of others. It is an expression of what we value most in ourselves and others. It is a frame of reference or way of looking at things.

Second, trust is a measure of our self-esteem—that is, how we feel about ourselves. Without trust, we may give up hope. With too little of it, we may be more suspicious of others than is needed. When we have high self-esteem, we usually flourish and are more able to trust others. There is no pride with trust— only humility and grace. There is no arrogance—only the recognition that we all make mistakes.

Third, trust comes from the inside out. We must first be trustworthy, which means clarifying our values, learning new skills to support those values, and then behaving accordingly. I call this *trust competence*. The development of trust competence is perhaps the most critical challenge we face as individuals, teams, and organizations. Words are cheap. It is actions that determine if we can be trusted. One's trust competence is fairly easy to measure because it will be reflected in what others say about us. It will show up in the quality, character, and effectiveness of our relationships with them.

What does any of this have to do with business? Everything. If we are trustworthy, others will trust us. We will be credible. Our motives will not be questioned. Our decisions are less likely to be challenged. Our relationships with others will be genuine and authentic. With trust, teams will exceed expectations, risks will be taken, and breakthroughs in operating efficiencies will occur. Speed will be achieved.

The Trust Imperative

Like Alec, most people want to be trusted, taken at their word, and respected for the value they bring to their work. We also want to be able to trust others. It is the glue that binds our relationships together. In this sense, trust is a need that is *not* subject to debate. We must have it if our relationships are to work at the optimal level. Thus, we could think of trust as an imperative, a given in human nature, even a natural law. This means that as a truth governing our lives, trust is a need, a requirement for human interaction, and an organizing principle for human conduct in all kinds of settings. Why is this so? What makes trust an imperative? In Figure 3-1, we see the five elements of this trust imperative.

• *A biological need.* When we enter this world, trust in others is a biological necessity. At birth we are vulnerable, exposed, and at risk. We are not conscious of that vulnerability, but we trust that the two individuals who brought us into the world will honor and take care of us. If that does not happen, our ability to trust others, and possibly even our ability to trust ourselves, will be damaged. As we grow older, our biological need to trust others does not go away, but our level of trust will be shaped by those early experiences and subsequent events.

At work, if we find ourselves in a low-trust environment, our response may be one of fear. If there is a moderate degree of trust from management, we may work well, but probably not at optimum level. With higher levels of trust, we may exhibit confidence, even exuberance. But our ability to trust others will in large part be a function of how we have been treated and our ability to cope with the pressures of the workplace. Biological necessity becomes psychological reality.

• *A psychological requirement.* Psychologically, people need predictability, stability, consistency, and a sense of security. We need to know where we stand with others and what we can count on so we can do our work well. Some degree of predictability is an expectation many people have when they come to work. But constant changes in the workplace, behaviors of

Figure 3-1. Key elements of the trust imperative.

supervisors, or events that threaten our security, run counter to our fundamental need for stability, and can increase distrust.

In a workplace where there is a rapid rate of change or a high degree of insecurity, the workforce will tend to focus on actions and behaviors that increase job stability. Where there is predictability, respect, and confidence in the abilities of the workforce, even if there is constant change, the trust level will likely be higher. In a high-trust workplace, even if jobs may be changed or terminated, there will be open communications about it, actions will be taken to retain those jobs, and the workforce will be treated fairly. Psychological security helps provide a level of emotional well-being.

- *Emotional well-being.* Emotionally, most people work to achieve a level of well-being in their lives. This is a measure of how they feel about themselves. High levels of emotional well-being are indicated by feeling in "balance," "on top of the world," in charge of their circumstances. Low levels of well-being are usually signified by feeling stressed, out of control, or a victim of one's circumstances.

In workplaces where there is uncertainty, fear, or disrespect, there will be lower levels of well-being. High levels of conflict, frustration, distrust, or breakdowns in relationships compromise our trust for one another. In these situations, we are more likely to cope rather than exceed production targets. Where there is stability and safety, and our needs are respected, our sense of well-being will be higher, as will be our ability to trust others. Productivity will increase, and we will be more able to deal effectively with the stresses of speed and change.

- *A cornerstone of self-respect.* I was once asked, "To what do you attach your self-respect?" The answer probably does not rest with the "what," but with *how* we feel about ourselves—that is, that we are good and capable people worthy of respect. Our self-respect is the ground upon which we stand each day. We will have a positive sense of ourselves if others trust us and we can trust them. We will be more likely to feel affirmed for who we are. We will have a greater sense of control over the future, and will be more willing to contribute to others.

When people go to work, they bring whatever level of self-respect they have. There is nothing we can do about that. But we still have to work with them. It is critical that we understand the impact that various levels of self-respect can have on trust levels in the workplace so that we can create a workplace that has room for everyone.

Individuals who have low self-respect are likely to be more dependent on others for direction, more fearful, and may have a high need for approval. Higher than normal levels of distrust and conflict are expected as these individuals try to use the organization to meet their fundamental needs for acceptance. If they have a higher level of self-esteem, the challenge will be to focus their independence, energy, and leadership on workplace goals. Those people who have high trust levels will be challenged to motivate those who are less trusting. In all instances, levels of self-respect will help shape the effectiveness of our work relationships.

- *The foundation for relationships.* We are tied together by relationships. Without some modicum of trust, our relationships will be less than successful. Without trust, our relationships become merely transactions. So we enter our relationships somewhere along a continuum that reflects the degrees of trust we have in each other. Some people begin their relationships from a position of trust, with a belief that there is credibility and integrity. For some, there is even an expectation that the initial position should be trust—that actions will match words. Others enter into relationships from a position of distrust, requiring others to prove they can be trusted. Whatever the initial position, the degree of success in any relationship will be a function of the level of trust the individuals themselves create and nurture as well as in their work culture.

Where there are low levels of trust in the workplace, we will see broken relationships, high levels of conflicts, and low productivity. When the workplace demonstrates a moderate level of trust, work gets done with some level of effectiveness, but it is not optimal. When there is a crisis, people will pull together; but otherwise, people are kind, but not necessarily honest with one another. In a high-trust work environment, there is a level of honesty, candor, and respect that gives the workforce a sense that they matter to each other and the business. Their self-esteem is affirmed, and their creativity, innovation, and productivity are outstanding.

The goal in our journey is to build a high-trust workplace by making the trust imperative an ally in the search for speed. When we consider all five dimensions of this imperative, a high-trust workplace is one in which the workforce is respected and honored, where psychological safety is high, emotional well-being is in balance, and self-esteem assures the effective resolution of issues, collaboration, and service to others. It is a workplace where communications are open and effective relationships are recognized as the cornerstone of business success.

But what are the core values that constitute this level of trust? What does it mean to have high levels of trust?

Understanding Self-Trust

///

Alec did not feel very good about himself after his deal collapsed. Even though he had worked hard, he knew almost immediately after he began presenting the project that he was in trouble. He had waited until the last minute because he had little confidence in himself. Instead, he rested on his relationship with the president, the timing of the bid, and his persuasiveness to get the necessary approvals. It backfired, and one of the prices he paid was a true loss of confidence in himself—that is, his self-trust. He knew he had cut corners. He even knew that others knew. Now his challenge was to rebuild that confidence and to discover what it meant to have high self-trust.

///

Self-trust consists of five core values. The bottom line is that my self-trust comes from the inside out. I must start from inside myself, clarify my values, and become confident that they represent how I live my life. Let's look at each of these core values (see Figure 3-2).

Value 1: Self-Respect

Webster defines *self-respect* as "a regard for one's own standing or position." Alec had asked his colleagues to trust him. Given his education and background, he felt he deserved their trust. Accordingly, self-respect is the value that I have for myself. It does not need to be affirmed by others. It is a clear, authentic sense that I am worthy of the respect of others. Based on this strong sense of self, I will respect others and give them the benefit of the doubt. My view of the world, my ability to form and keep trust-based relationships, and my performance will in some way find its roots in the degree of self-respect I have.

Figure 3-2. The core values of self-trust.

We usually have high levels of self-respect when we have been respected by others from our earliest years, when our bio-logical, psychological, and emotional needs have been met. We were listened to, honored, celebrated, and taught about the world. Alternatively, we have low self-respect when we have had good reason to feel insecure or have found ourselves victims of circumstances. We may have learned that the world was not a place to be trusted, that we could be hurt, and that we have to compensate for that. To compensate, we may have become arrogant, aggressive, or defensive.

In organizations that are led and managed by people who have high levels of self-respect, there is high value placed on relationships. There is a sense of security and a belief that nearly all problems can be solved. In low-performing organizations, the leader with high self-respect will get the workforce focused on a new vision, mission, and strategic direction.

In organizations led by people with low levels of self-respect, the workforce is fearful, isolated, and focused on just getting the work done. The probabilities of conflict are much higher as people's own insecurities are magnified in a workplace defined by insecurity. Defensiveness and reactive behaviors will more likely occur in this type of work environment.

Self-respect is not something I *do*. It is not something we can *get* by going to a workshop. It is something I *have*, and we all have it to some degree or another. It is critical, however, that we are aware of the key role it plays in defining our capacity to trust others.

Value 2: Full Responsibility and Accountability

Full responsibility is an individual act of commitment. It means that we are fully responsible for our values, beliefs, and behaviors. To be *fully* accountable means we accept the consequences of those behaviors, and if necessary, make it right. Full responsibility and accountability come from a strong sense of self, of one's competence, and a realistic sense that the trials in life can be successfully negotiated. People trust those who are fully responsible and who are willing to be held accountable for their actions, as well as their words.

///

Alec had ambitions to rise within Antac, and his colleagues knew this. But he did not take full responsibility for the approval process for the deal he was negotiating. He waited until the last moment to bring it to a decision. His colleagues felt manipulated and challenged the process, and the result was failure. Alec was held accountable, not only by his teammates for his approach but also by his superiors. It did not take long for the president to hear about what happened. He saw a character flaw and decided not to promote Alec.

///

Full responsibility and accountability are critical indicators of one's level of self-trust. People with high levels of self-trust do not need to play games to get a decision made or a process implemented. They own their jobs, understand their strengths and limitations, and engage others to get work done. If there are breakdowns, they deal directly with the individuals responsible. If they are responsible for the breakdown, they own up to it, take the heat, and learn from the experience. People who are not fully responsible and accountable are usually not trusted. When put into positions of leadership in an organization, there is usually crisis, conflict, and a breakdown in performance.

Organizations that are fully responsible and accountable have clearly defined roles and responsibilities, are proactive in the marketplace, plan ahead, engage their customers, have systems in place to ensure effective implementation, and are not afraid of receiving feedback. These types of businesses will find they have high levels of customer satisfaction and performance.

Value 3: Honor and Dignity

Semper Fi, as the U.S. Marines motto, symbolizes honor, dignity, and high levels of self-trust. It means something to be a Marine. Honor is a mark of distinction, one's reputation, and the regard that others have for us—our reputation. Dignity is how persons of honor hold themselves. To have honor and dignity is to have high self-trust, as measured by our actions, words, and training, as well as by the regard that others have for us.

Was Alec an honorable man? Did his conduct have dignity? Or was he just trying to get a bid approved? In his race to become the next senior vice-president, he lost sight of the bigger picture. In this transaction, his actions betrayed his real intent. To act with honor might have meant focusing on what was best for the company, planning the meeting well in advance of the deadline, fully disclosing all aspects of the deal to his teammates, soliciting input, and then letting the chips fall where they may.

People with high levels of honor and dignity stand out. They are trusted. For example, in MarCap, a Fortune 500 company, the chief operating officer, Andrew, was the person everyone sought for advice. They knew, and said, that Andrew had only the best interests of the company at heart. He had no personal agenda. He was a diplomat, a statesman, a man of honor. You could always count on Andrew to do the right thing for the company. In contrast, people who are viewed as having low levels of honor and dignity, if in positions of leadership, are more likely than not to compromise the mission of the company for individual gain.

An Honorable Leader Resigns

The handwriting had been on the wall for several months. The business's performance data was not what the Board required, the morale of the workforce was at an all-time low, and Jack's senior leadership team was increasingly restless. Attempts to bring in new programs or cut costs, to restructure or get new blood into the organization simply was not working. The message back to Jack was that it was his approach to leadership that everyone considered to be the problem.

The meeting had been set by the Board Chairman to discuss next steps. When challenged by his team, Jack got defensive. He saw the numbers and figured it was more politics than reality. The Chairman systematically began to address each and every one of the issues raised by the team. After four hours, it became increasingly clear that there was really only one solution. Jack asked for a one-day recess.

The next day, there was no need for the team to meet. Out of respect for his team, the Chairman, and the company, Jack tendered his resignation citing his duty and obligation to uphold the principles of the company.

Organizations with high levels of honor and dignity consistently show up on the list of America's "most admired companies." Their reputations are clear and above reproach. For example, a pharmaceutical company that experienced drug tampering subsequently recalled the product and helped the people adversely affected by the drug. In another example, a toy company that soon realized that a newly released, hot-selling toy had parts that could choke small children not only recalled the product, but also redesigned the processes that led to its release. Doing the right thing is not just about short-term profits; in fact, doing the right thing might result in short-term losses. Doing the right thing is about a company's long-term reputation for trust, honor, and integrity.

Value 4: Integrity

Webster has defined *integrity* as "the firm adherence to a code of moral values." Put another way, people are seen as having high integrity when their actions match their words, as well as their intent. If there is honor, dignity, full responsibility, accountability, and self-respect, there is a greater likelihood of high integrity. A breach in the integrity of an individual, team, or organization occurs when there is belief that the truth is not being told, where there is sleight of hand, or if someone is trying to achieve a gain at someone else's expense. Alec's actions, by this definition, were viewed as a breach of integrity. He was out only for himself and was willing to put his own needs above those of the company.

Achieving and maintaining a high level of integrity is extremely difficult to do in a transaction-based corporation, which typically values results and efficiency over process. It is even more difficult to achieve a high-integrity work culture when individual success is measured by how well an individual executes transactions rather than who that person is. As Alec learned, without a high level of integrity, there can be no trust, and without trust, his relationships became no more than transactions. Once Alec's integrity was called into question, it was a long road back. With his integrity diminished, so too was his credibility.

Value 5: Credibility

There are two types of credibility: *external* credibility, or that which we give to others; and *internal* credibility, or our belief in ourselves. Both types of credibility come from within us as an expression of our own confidence and respect.

- *External credibility.* When it seems like nothing is working, to whom do we turn? Most likely it will be someone we can trust, someone who is credible. What makes someone credible—whether it is Walter Cronkite or John Glenn—is our belief in that person's integrity and our confidence in his or her purposeful, positive intent. Credibility is the faith we put in others, a measure of our confidence in who they are, their abilities, and their understanding. It is our unflinching belief that they will do the right thing and can be counted on, especially when the chips are down. We give a person credibility when we consistently see that their words and actions match up. In addition, most of us have a "sixth sense" about whether someone is considered credible—it is intuitive.

When there is an inconsistent pattern of behavior, when we doubt a person's motives or intent, or when we believe lies or half-truths have been told, we self-correct, make adjustments in our judgments about that person's trustworthiness, and then behave accordingly. This adjustment process is almost automatic.

• *Internal credibility*. How many times have we said, "If you want something done right, do it yourself"? This is an expression of our belief in ourselves, that we have confidence in our own abilities to get the job done. It is also an expression of our lack of confidence in others. Internal credibility is knowing we can count on ourselves, especially in the face of adversity.

By these definitions, Alec had little external credibility among his teammates. His motives were suspect. He was out for himself, at the expense of others. This made challenging his numbers, assumptions, and time frames essential to protect the company from a risky investment. His internal credibility was more bravado than substance. He pushed the case and the schedule to get the decision he needed.

As with integrity, achieving high levels of credibility takes time. It comes from a consistent set of behaviors, guided by a set of positive values, that are expressed over a long period of time. When a business leader or manager has high credibility, people in the workplace are motivated to act, to go beyond the routine. They will work to exceed expectations out of respect for that leader. They are trusted. Credibility is much easier to lose than to gain, and when lost, it is almost impossible to regain. For example, the president of a major national bank was acquiring another bank that had invested heavily in foreign markets. The extent of this investment, more than a billion dollars, was not fully disclosed to the acquiring bank's shareholders until after they had voted on the deal. When one of those foreign investments went sour and the stock dropped by 10 percent, the U.S. Congress decided to investigate, and a raft of shareholder suits showed up overnight. The president was fired by the board. His credibility could not be restored. Trust-based relationships require credibility.

Trust and Performance

Alec's self-trust had received a body blow, not just from the failed deal but also by what that deal represented: an aspiring young business leader who was willing to put his own interests ahead of his team, his company, and ultimately the customer. At least he recognized that he had violated the values of self-trust, although the initial damage had been done. In his experience, we have seen how his self-trust was tied to performance. We saw how his character flaw affected his relationships with his colleagues.

Our self-trust is how we are known. It shapes how we lead and manage, and therefore is the basis for the performance of our organizations. What we see in Figure 3-3 is a summary analysis of the relationship between leadership self-trust and organizational performance, and the types of actions leaders are likely to take, given their level of trust. Alec found himself in Quadrant III. The goal is to find ourselves in Quadrant I.

• *Quadrant I: High self-trust/high performance.* In this quadrant, relationships are essential to these leaders; there is a sense of security; they focus on results; planning is proactive; they build value and ownership, and solve problems effectively. Conflicts are dealt with directly and efforts are made to prevent

Figure 3-3. Leadership self-trust and organizational performance.

		ORGANIZATIONAL PERFORMANCE	
		High	Low
LEADERSHIP SELF-TRUST	High	**Quadrant I** • Relationships essential • High security • Focus on results • Proactive • Problem-solving • Direct dealings • Act in interest of organization	**Quadrant II** • Crisis • Low security • Inspire by vision; mobilize workforce • Reactive planning to stabilize • Conflicts as opportunities to change • Act to ensure stability of workforce
	Low	**Quadrant III** • Transactions important • Leader is insecure • Leader-based planning • Limited ownership • Nice, but not honest • Act in interest of turf/silo	**Quadrant IV** • Crisis management • High insecurity; anxiety • Conflicts everywhere • Dysfunctional behavior • No planning; frantic • Blaming & shaming • Act in best interest of self

them in the future. On balance, these leaders will always do the right thing in the interest of the organization.

• *Quadrant II: High self-trust/low performance.* In this quadrant, the focus is on challenges and even crises to be addressed. There is insecurity owing to low performance. These leaders will mobilize the workforce and inspire through a shared vision and mission. Planning will be reactive at first, but will then stabilize. Conflicts are addressed as symptoms of larger issues, and problems are seen as opportunities to change. On balance, these leaders will do what is necessary to ensure the stability of the workforce.

• *Quadrant III: Low self-trust/high performance.* In this quadrant, transactions are more important than relationships to its leaders. The organization is doing well, but the leader is viewed as insecure. Planning will be limited and tied to the leader's agenda; a close group of confidants will advise the leader, meaning that ownership is limited. Conflicts tend to be personalized, while there is a tendency to be nice, but not honest. On balance, these leaders will do what is right to preserve their turf.

• *Quadrant IV: Low self-trust/low performance.* In this quadrant, crises and feelings of insecurity are frequent. The workforce is fearful and anxious. Conflicts are everywhere. Dysfunctional behavior shows up in many ways, including arrogance and distrust. Planning does not happen; it is a highly reactive environment, even frantic. Finger-pointing and a very active rumor mill are ways people displace responsibility for breakdowns. This is not a fun or nice place to work, and the leader's low self-trust merely reinforces that sense across the organization. On balance, in this type of situation, these leaders will do what is best for themselves.

When leaders bring high self-trust to their organizations, they inspire the workforce to high performance and greater speed, even in the face of adversity, rapid change, or instability. If these values are in place in an organization, trust becomes the cornerstone of its culture. Fear is routed out. *Respect, honor,* and *dignity* become the watchwords. If Alec had had high self-trust, it would not have mattered to his teammates whether he was in Buenos Aires or Oshkosh; they would have known they could count on him. The teleconference, if needed at all, would have been short and focused on the terms of the deal, and the deal would have been successfully closed.

In Closing

The point of this chapter is that strengthening individual self-trust has a direct bearing on organizational performance. It comes from the inside out. It reflects the reality of the trust imperative, and a recognition that trust is a natural law. It would be ideal if all leaders were in Quadrant I. But, like Alec, most of us do not operate at this optimum level of self-trust. We are human. We make mistakes. We have backgrounds and experiences that may have compromised our ability to trust ourselves and others.

Similarly, most organizations do not operate at such a high level of trust. They are dynamic, changing systems of individuals, each of whom is trying to find a way to bring meaning to his life and value to the workplace. If the workplace culture is based on the values of self-trust, however, there will be a greater likelihood that the organization itself will be in Quadrant I.

By itself, trust is a difficult principle to understand. But in the context of leading a business at the speed of change, it takes on additional importance. If ever there was a defining quality for business success, it is trust. If ever there was a time to embed this principle permanently in our corporate character and culture, it is now. The key to success can be found in creating an organizational framework based on the principle of trust. We will be able to lead our businesses at the speed of change if we can evolve toward this framework—a relationship-based corporation.

4

//

The Relationship-Based Corporation

"Our challenge is to create work environments fit for the human spirit."

—Merlin Walberg, business consultant

//

"The pig is getting near the end of the snake" was how Warren, the president of MSI, opened the first of three senior management retreats, *"and I intend for us to be a part of that market."* He was referring to the billions in investment dollars that baby boomers were turning over to the next generation. Warren then issued this challenge: *"We must reorganize, get flatter, and be driven by the customer. And we must do this by yesterday."* His strategic concern was that this eighty-year-old financial institution was too internally focused, too slow, and not effectively organized to meet the competitive challenges coming from all sides—insurance companies, national and regional brokerage houses, Internet services, credit card companies, and a host of other financial service businesses.

Warren went on to outline the very real threat to the company's profitability over the next two years. If there was not a quick response from the company, its twenty years of steady earnings growth would begin to decline, and with it, the company's personal financial futures. The company was already beginning to see some erosion of its customer base. There were *even rumors the company might be acquired, as consolidation in the industry accelerated. Time was of the essence. He challenged his team to give him a turnaround plan he could implement within nine months.*

The senior management team quickly realized the complexity of this task. MSI was steeped in tradition. How could a business with such a history and 3,000 employees possibly change this fast? It was a transaction-based business, which had held fast to the command approach to leadership. There were ten layers of hierarchy between Warren and the front-line service provider. Communications were one-way and infrequent. The company's approach to customer service was driven by the products and services it had to offer. A "we know what is best for you" culture was very much at work. Portfolio managers were encouraged to compete against each other. Their silos were guarded carefully, leaving customers to fend for themselves if they wanted to access services in other parts of the company.

The management style at MSI was based essentially on compliance. People did what they had to in order to get the job done. Conflicts existed, but were never resolved. Politics and rumors were the main fare. You did not challenge the status quo unless you wanted to have a different career track. Responsibility flowed down while accountability was from the bottom up. The level of fear was palpable but rarely discussed. All the right things were being said about teamwork, but the reality was that it was just talk. This was a "program of the month" workplace. If you waited long enough, the program would go away.

This series of senior management retreats had been designed to begin addressing these concerns head-on, first by tackling the strategic business issues and then by developing an organizational system that would transform how the company operated so it could compete in the new marketplace.

In the face of MSI's very real need for speed, its traditional, transaction-based approach to work could not be changed fast enough. Intellectually, the senior managers knew that a trust-based workplace, which is flat, team-based, and highly collaborative, was the best way to work. They knew that the best way to serve customers was to put them in the driver's seat. They knew that the many programs they had tried in the past to address these concerns had met with only limited success.

What the MSI team did not know was that to create a truly customer-driven, team-based, and trust-centered organization that could respond quickly to the market, would require a fundamental change in the organizational system. New technologies would not fix it. Training programs would not make it happen. Restructuring into teams by itself would not meet the need for more effective work relationships. What they soon came to realize was that to transform the business to meet the market crisis, they would need a new way to work. Based on the principle of trust, this new approach would, over time, enable them to dismantle the transaction-based system and evolve toward what I will call a relationship-based corporation.

The senior managers at MSI began to ask questions like: What is a relationship-based corporation? How does it work? How is it different from the transaction-based approach to work? Once the evolution has occurred, what real difference would it make? The purpose of this chapter, then, is to describe the overall framework for this next step in corporate evolution. To begin, we will define the new covenant, or agreement, that will govern the relationship between management and the workforce. Then we will take a detailed look at defining the seven key elements of a relationship-based corporation: customer, culture, vision, leadership, people and business processes, structure, and outcomes. In subsequent chapters we will look at the methodology and implementation processes needed to create and sustain this new approach to work.

The New Covenant

"Treat others as ends, never as means."
—From *Markings* by Dag Hammarskjöld, former
Secretary General of the United Nations

The former Secretary General's statement is as true today as it was in his time. People and their relationships are the key to business success. A future of speed and adaptability requires us to view our relationships as the end, whereas the products we produce or the services we render are merely milestones along the way. We have only begun to evolve toward that future by realizing that all the other approaches to trust, speed, and high performance are not very effective. To continue that evolution, we must create a new psychological contract, or covenant, between the workforce and management—one that is tailored to the knowledge era.

In the past, the psychological contract was essentially an exchange. An employee would be hired for a specific set of skills or capabilities in exchange for a wage. An employee was viewed as a resource, a cost, and a means to an end. For the individual worker, the contract was a trade-off—where people gave their loyalty, energy, and capabilities to a company, often for life, and in return received compensation, benefits, and some job security. High performers were rewarded with promotion. High performance meant stability. But this was not a work environment that welcomed challenges or conflicts in the workforce. Compliance was the key to success. Management was humane, but when there was a choice between the corporation's bottom line and the individual's need, the bottom line always was chosen.

All that needs to change. The entire workforce-management relationship has been changed by market forces, new technologies, higher levels of workforce awareness, and the need for speed. To realize the benefits of speed in a networked marketplace, we must have a covenant that enables the work relationship to be one of trust, respect, integrity, and honor. It must be a relationship owned by all parties and not just a contract the employee must accept.

A *workplace covenant* is usually an assumed agreement between management and the workforce that spells out their understandings about the trade-offs between risk, skills, labor, and rewards. It also delineates the ways in which the parties will treat each other. Sometimes these are positive agreements, but often they lead to conflict.

In a relationship-based corporation, the covenant frames the character, quality, and integrity of the work relationship. It is not just a piece of paper but rather a binding obligation that is manifested in our behavior toward one another and in the company's management operating system. The quality of this covenant will reflect our underlying beliefs about human nature, the key drivers in the business, and how management and the workforce address rapid change. There are five key attributes of this new covenant around which work is conducted in a relationship-based corporation:

1. It recognizes and implements the trust imperative.
2. It is a mirror of our self-trust.
3. It must be mutually defined.
4. It must be managed for efficacy.
5. It matures from learning; it is not static.

This new covenant is more than a set of expectations that are negotiated among the parties. It is a set of *rights and obligations* people have toward each other in the new workplace, rights and obligations that are mutually defined and agreed to. It is a new common ground. Let's look at each of these attributes in depth.

Implements the Trust Imperative

A relationship-based covenant recognizes the fundamental need people have for trust—that it is a natural law. Accordingly, the company's approach to people will be based on a belief in the inherent goodness of people. Systems will be built to nurture their growth and development rather than focus on control. There will be little or no need for thick policy manuals, strict procedures, or adversarial contracts. Organized labor unions will not need to exist. People's basic economic and respect needs will be met. Teams will be created, trained, and nurtured. Relationships will be built across the company, with little or no need for levels, titles, or walls. People will be known for their expertise, skills, and ability to lead when needed. The focus of the workforce will be external rather than internal. The emphasis will be on the customers and leveraging the intellectual and human capital of the company to meet their needs. Everyone will be involved in helping shape the company's future. There will be no need for silos or compartmentalization. Instead, the structure will be flat, adaptive, and fast.

Mirrors Our Self-Trust

This new covenant will honor the self-respect and dignity of each individual, in terms of not only his or her skills and competencies but also their needs, hopes, expectations, and abilities to grow and learn. It will recognize that people come to work from a variety of backgrounds, with different levels of self-esteem and different skill sets. Accordingly, it will support processes that build pride, identity, and competence. Full participation in the company's success will mean an increased sense of ownership in the company's mission and a high degree of alignment with its vision and strategic direction. The focus will be on service, meeting customer needs, learning new skills, and interpersonal effectiveness.

The new covenant is not about pay and benefits. It is about relationship and contribution. Therefore, performance can be measured by customers and peers as well as through self-assessments. The roles of the "supervisor" and control mechanisms like time clocks will gradually disappear as people learn how to hold themselves accountable. Job classifications and succession ladders will no longer be as important since teams of people with the required skills, regardless of where they are in the company, will be brought together to get the job done. Having effective teaming skills and behavior will become a prerequisite for being hired. Promotions upward will become much less important as the focus shifts from external rewards to internal development. The emphasis in this covenant is on knowledge and growth.

Is Mutually Defined

This covenant will be mutually defined and redefined over time between management and the workforce. There will be a recognition that, in order for the business to have vitality, there must be mutuality—that is, an understanding of the value that each individual brings to the organization. Contracts may not be needed, but if they are, they will be discussed rather than predetermined. Similarly, the most effective ways to meet market requirements or customer needs will be mutually defined by the members of the workforce involved.

Pay will be based on performance, skills, customer value, interpersonal effectiveness, and/or growth rather than on some strict formula. In a relationship-based corporation, performance reviews are for everyone and are the basis for building mutual understanding of what the company needs to change.

Managed for Efficacy

The essence of this new covenant is its ability to redefine the working relationships between management and the workforce in a way that builds trust. One expression of this new level of trust is to move a company's culture from a focus on "I," or the values promoting individual advancement at the expense of the group, to a culture of "We," where the whole is greater than the sum of the parts and where unity is valued over personality. To this end, the covenant must be managed for efficacy—that is, so that it is everyone's responsibility to ensure the success of the agreement. While teams have a governance process that provides for internal accountability, efficacy is about intent. It is the intent of every member to honor the spirit of the covenant. This may mean calling another to account or surfacing issues people do not want to talk about. But ultimately, without efficacy and accountability, there can be no integrity; without integrity there can be no trust.

Matures From Learning

While the underlying principles of the covenant will remain, its applications will change as the workforce learns how to operate differently and matures. The covenant, in this sense, is a living expression of the values of those who commit to it. As people and circumstances change, as the company matures in its implementation of the covenant, it is important that there be a periodic review, revision, and recommitment to its provisions. More important, growth from learning is an implicit expectation. The covenant's effectiveness and adaptability will be stopped only by the limits we put on it.

At the MSI retreat, senior managers used these five attributes to develop what they called their "Workplace Covenant," an expression of their commitment to create a relationship-based workplace:

The MSI Workplace Covenant

- Our people are the source of our strength. Our first priority is to them so that we may meet our customers' needs. Should the business ever be at risk, we will put the needs of the workforce and the customer first.
- Trust is the glue that holds us together. We will do everything we can to establish and enhance our trust of each other.
- We believe the whole is greater than the sum of its parts.
- We will honor each individual while committing to become a "We."
- We commit to equality. No one person is better than another.
- We will consider each person's contribution with respect.
- Perception is reality; we commit to creating a shared perception of reality.
- We are all responsible and accountable for our success.
- We will periodically review, renew, and recommit to our covenant.

Recognizing that the covenant needed to be put into specific terms people could understand, the senior management team worked with a representative group of employees to develop a set of workplace "rights and obligations" that set parameters and boundaries for individual and group conduct. Their results were as follows:

Every Member of MSI Has the Following Workplace Rights

- To be trusted, respected, and honored. Abuse will not be tolerated.
- To be fairly treated in all aspects of work.

- Integrity in how this business conducts itself.
- To be treated ethically and responsibly.
- To participate in all aspects of business operations and to be involved in decision making.
- To participate in the development of one's own future.
- To have full communications and an open-book approach to management.

Every Member of MSI Has the Following Workplace Obligations

- To tell the truth at all times.
- To fully participate in the conduct of the business. Sitting on the sidelines is not acceptable.
- To be fully responsible for the success of the business as well as one's job.
- To collaborate effectively with others.
- To learn from one's mistakes and grow.
- To be held accountable for one's words and actions.

With their covenant, rights, and obligations in place, the MSI management team prepared to create the framework for their relationship-based corporation.

Defining the Relationship-Based Corporation

"It's not about technology or structure; it's about relationships."

—Bill Smithson, information technology manager

"I know relationships are important," Jeff said as he met with his MSI teammates about their new organizational design. "But we've always had relationships. I think the key question here is their quality and how we create a workplace where trust, quality, and speed can be achieved. People make our business work, not our processes or technology. We need to design a system that will work for them."

In a relationship-based corporation, it is the character and quality of work relationships that ensure the success of the business. Speed comes from trust-based relationships. The challenge is to create an organizational system that understands, supports, and nurtures those relationships.

Let's define what this type of corporation is, the critical elements of its system, and what types of results it can produce.

Webster has defined *relation* as "the attitude or stance which two or more persons or groups assume toward one another." When applied to a work setting, *relationship* could be defined as the attitude people have toward working with each other. When applied to work in this context, we can define a relationship-based corporation this way:

///

A relationship-based corporation is an organizational system based on the principle of trust, whose leadership and workforce are aligned on a common vision and whose processes and structure are driven by the mutual respect of the members, the integrity of the business, and the value added to the customer.

///

This type of business processes all the same information, decisions, and problems as the transaction-based company; however, its emphasis is not on the task but on the quality of the relationships maintained in fulfilling the task. The task gets completed, but not by putting the work relationship at risk.

In a principle-based organization dedicated to serving the customer, people are treated as an end. They are recognized as the true source of energy, quality, and commitment for the business. Systems, technologies, and tools are mere means to the end. At the end of the day, in a relationship-based workplace, the only true asset a business has is its people, their intellectual capital, and the value their relationships add to their customers.

A Framework for the Relationship-Based Corporation

A relationship-based corporation is governed by a workplace covenant similar to the one developed by MSI. It has a set of workplace rights and obligations to which each member of the business subscribes. And all of this operates within a system that orchestrates the linkages and interactions among the company's customers, culture, vision, leadership, processes, structure, and results. Figure 4-1 shows how these key organizational elements relate to each other. In the balance of this chapter I will describe each element in terms of how it is manifested in a relationship-based corporation.

Customer-Driven

We begin by acknowledging the central role that the customer plays in any business. In a relationship-based company, the

Figure 4-1. The relationship-based corporation.

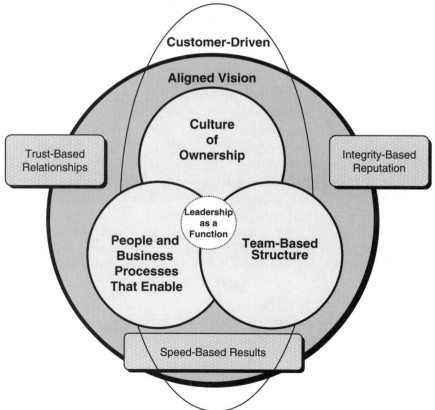

needs of the customer drive the types of products or services the company develops and delivers. A key distinction here is between companies that are customer-focused and those that are customer-driven. In a customer-focused company like MSI, the importance of customers is acknowledged, but the message to customers is essentially "We know what is best for you." This type of company tends to be internally focused. New products and services find their origin in the capabilities and competencies of the company, get modified to meet some of the customer's needs, and are then justified to the customer as being in their best interest. Customer satisfaction surveys, if conducted at all, are not likely to challenge the underlying assumptions of how the company works.

On the other hand, a customer-driven, relationship-based company is externally focused. In terms of the goods and services created to meet market demand, the company conducts extensive market research, engages the customers in frequent needs assessments, develops prototypes and trials on new products, and aggressively evaluates the value added. Here the relationship is characterized by an attitude of "What else do you need?" Formal customer partnerships may be developed that define the nature of the working relationships they will have, which in turn can lead to a higher degree of trust. Specifically this might mean that there is a single point of focus between the customer and the company. It might also involve a cross-functional team of key players essential to the customer's success.

A partnering agreement can specify how the partners will work together. As part of that agreement, a governance process can be put in place to develop agreements for how the partners will handle the critical functions of planning, decision making, communications, problem solving, and conflict resolution. The company's performance review system can, in part, include customer assessments of its service, quality, and attitude. This level of accountability can transform this relationship into one that is customer driven. Customers are not just companies who buy services—they are the business.

A Culture of Ownership

The culture of any company represents what it considers to be important. In a relationship-based company, the alignment of the leadership and the workforce around its culture involves a set of core values and beliefs, and a set of operating principles that go to the heart of what the business is about. At its most fundamental level, the company's culture will determine the speed at which the company is able to move, for it is in the culture that the level of organizational trust is created and sustained. There are four ways to define a relationship-based corporation's culture.

1. *Core principles and beliefs.* The principles, values, and beliefs of a relationship-based company are about trust, respect, ownership, alignment, responsibility, accountability, and integrity. At the heart of its operations is the principle of collaboration. The focus of the workforce is on learning how to collaborate inside so that they can compete outside. Both management and the workforce live the principles. They are more than slogans. These core principles are the final arbiter, the supreme court for how key decisions are made. They are ingrained in the workforce, and there are clear expectations about how these values will show up in behavior, work processes, and organizational structure.

2. *Corporate identity, style, and heritage.* Every company has an identity, a style, and a history. In a relationship-based workplace, the company is known for putting its people and customers first. It goes the extra mile to ensure the stability and security of the workforce. It has a strong commitment to quality and integrity. The style of the organization reflects its overall approach to dealing with its people and customers. For example, it may have a "cowboy culture," or it may be seen as bureaucratic. In a relationship-based company, the style is authentic, meaning that it is honest, direct, open, and focused on solving problems. The heritage of any company is its legacy—its beginnings, evolution, and the changes it has made to keep pace with the times. Creating a common language becomes a way the company builds and sustains a shared perception of reality. Its customs and habits also define its character and provide a common reference point for pride and self-esteem.

3. *Character.* This is how the company is viewed by its workforce, including its core values, credibility and integrity, its

---

Putting the Internal Customer in Charge

Ever since this steel company had been formed, corporate head-quarters had always set the standards for how the plants would operate. With the industry in decline, and this company seeing a steep drop in revenues in the last ten years, the senior leadership decided to experiment. The plant managers had been saying for some time that the company's $1.3 billion supply and logistics function needed to be streamlined and reorganized to increase savings. The current system did not meet their needs.

A twelve-member cross-functional team, including two plant managers, was formed to address this problem. This was a new approach. Never before had corporate delegated such a delicate issue to the plants. But they figured that this new level of ownership just might do the trick.

In their meetings, the team described the "current state" implications of the company's centralized approach to the business. In their "future state" they defined the core values and principles they wanted the business to be run by. They redesigned the supply and logistics function using that framework, and put the plant managers in charge of the supply and logistics budget.

When the report was presented to the CEO and his key staff, he applauded the team's effort in the beginning to reverse a cultural direction that was driving the company out of business. In the ensuing months, fully 25 percent of the supply and logistics costs were reduced by the plant managers—dollars that flowed directly to the bottom line.

---

pride and honor, its level of professionalism and maturity, its ability to learn and grow, and its ability to change effectively. In a relationship-based company, the business has high ratings on all counts, is a learning organization, and has invested heavily in its ability to adapt and change behavior, processes, and systems to meet the needs of the market.

4. *Energy and commitment.* This fourth element of a company's culture is the most elusive and yet the most critical. It is

the energy and commitment of the workforce. This is reflected in morale, attitude, productivity levels, loyalty, initiative, creativity, and the quality of work completed. In a relation-based workplace, there is a high level of energy, with 80 percent of the workforce saying consistently that they are working at 80 percent or more of their capacity.

The cultural evolution a company experiences is from a compliance and transaction-based approach to work, where power and personality drive the processes and structure of the business, to this principle-based approach to work, a covenant based on mutual trust, and a set of rights and obligations that ensures a high degree of involvement and accountability.

An Aligned Vision

The central nervous system of any organization is the degree of alignment that exists throughout the workforce on a wide range of critical issues. Like the control exercised by the central nervous system over the body, the ability of any company to marshal and leverage its resources depends on the degree to which the company invests in its market, customers, workforce, and culture to realize its own destiny. In a relationship-based corporation, this is achieved through a high degree of involvement and participation by leadership, the workforce, and customers in setting the course of the company. This is achieved in the following ways:

- *Market alignment.* The company is strategically positioned relative to its competitors, its unique and value-added role is clear, and its strategic direction is focused. For example, MSI leadership knew that if they did not meet the investment needs of the baby-boomers, they could lose significant market share, and possibly even be acquired.

- *Customer alignment.* Customer partnerships provide key inputs into the market alignment process. Their specific needs become the core of what the business does in the future. For example, Warren knew all too well that they were an internally focused company. They told the customers what MSI would sell them. Now that would be turned around.

• *Workforce alignment.* The first level is awareness, so that everyone in the business understands what the business is about, its vision, goals, and overall direction. The second level is engaging them in a dialogue concerning the direction the business is taking, and eliciting their input and recommendations. A third level of alignment involves delegating the alignment process and opening it up to new interpretations and perspectives as the strategy is implemented. A fourth and final level of alignment is when everyone in the business can say they "own" it, that it is theirs. The involvement of MSI's senior management was just the first step in this redirection of the business. Warren had asked two of his closest aides to help design a dialogue, which would align everyone.

• *Cultural alignment.* This involves ensuring that the processes, structures, and strategic focus of the business are congruent with the culture of the business. Incongruence results in breakdowns, misalignment, and eventually poor performance and mistrust. Warren also knew that MSI's incentive system would need to change. It was focused on rewarding individuals. He knew the new focus on teams would require team-based incentives.

The critical ingredient in this evolution is the role of leadership, whose primary role is the facilitation of this entire alignment process.

Leadership as a Function

Gone are the days when business leadership is the exclusive domain of the senior executive. Increasingly, business leaders are realizing that the heroic leader, the charismatic leader, or the influence leader creates a level of dependence that keeps others from taking responsibility for the success of the business. In a relationship-based corporation, leadership is a function, not a position. Whether it is used depends often upon the situation, the expertise or skills required, and the individual's willingness and capacity to exercise that leadership. In this new approach to work, business leadership takes on three important, and different, dimensions: responsibility, collaboration, and transformation.

1. *Responsible leadership.* It is the job of responsible leadership, wherever it may be in the company, to encourage every member of the workforce to be fully responsible and accountable for the success of the business. Responsible leadership means building independence within the workforce—that is, the ability to make decisions and solve problems at the lowest level possible. Responsible leadership means fostering interdependence among teams, suppliers, and customers. Responsible leadership results in the lines and walls disappearing between silos, departments, levels, and perceived degrees of power. Responsible leadership values integrity and credibility. Every effort is made to "walk-the-talk," and then to "teach-the-walk." Results still matter, but they are results in terms of business performance, relationship effectiveness, and the company's reputation. In a relationship-based corporation, everyone has the potential of being a responsible leader.

2. *Collaborative leadership.* How responsible leaders lead is through the skillful application of collaborative work principles and practices. With their actions based on the core values of ownership, alignment, respect, and responsibility, collaborative leaders are facilitative rather than authoritative. Their goal is to increase the level of self-trust in every member of the workforce, to tap into everyone's hidden productivity, to release everyone's full potential, and to build a strong sense of ownership in the business. They engage the workforce in making critical business decisions and solving business problems. The collaborative leader understands that people drive the business rather than technology, strategy, finance, or shareholders. This type of leader hones people and process skills in meetings, teams, conflict resolution, and change management. The collaborative leader learns to sponsor people's success.

3. *Transformational leadership.* In addition to ensuring that customer needs are met and that the workforce is attaining its full potential, transformational leadership recognizes that organizations change over time and ensures that the organiza-

tional system also evolves in a way that sustains productivity and adds value for customers. Transformational leaders are never satisfied with the status quo, either within themselves or in their organizations. They are constantly searching the horizon, analyzing trends, listening to the work environment, and engaging the workforce in adapting the organization's processes, structures, and systems to meet the new needs. They know that transformation comes from the inside out, both for themselves and for their businesses. Transformational leaders understand that true, lasting change comes through ownership and responsibility, and that it is evolutionary, not revolutionary.

The structure of leadership in a relationship-based corporation reflects an emphasis on dialogue, exchange, and interaction. Communications in the leadership team flow in all directions. Everyone's opinion has equal merit. The emphasis is on open dialogue and honest and candid discussion of critical issues, rather than on politics, hidden agendas, or ego-based solutions. Relationship-based leadership teams are concerned about the expectations, perceptions, and morale of the workforce. Decisions are made based on what is best not only for the customer and the shareholders but also for the workforce. There is a focus on process as well as results.

With the culture, vision, and leadership elements in place, the people and work processes of a relationship-based corporation are designed to be enablers. They ensure that customer needs, the company's vision, the management operating system, and business results are achieved in a way that reflects the core principles and beliefs of the organization.

People Processes

There are three aspects of people processes that enable trust and speed: team competence, skills development, and learning behavior.

1. *Team competence*. Members of the workforce will have a high degree of competence in team governance. In order for teams of coworkers to be successful, they need a front-loaded,

collaborative governance process that enables them to set the rules of behavior. This goes beyond the traditional process of "forming-norming-storming-performing" because many teams never get beyond the storming stage. In the collaborative team process, members consent to a set of operating agreements and a charter with clear roles and responsibilities that enable them to build a high level of trust on the front end so that they can increase their speed once the work is under way. In terms of project management, the workforce knows how to set up a project management process involving people across the business and that ensures that stakeholder needs are satisfied. They have internal management processes that enable them to network, adjust, adapt, and change as needed by the customer or business process. Finally, they have trouble-shooting capabilities that enable them to sense problems and issues, make the necessary interventions, and solve the problems.

2. *Skills development.* Members of a relationship-based corporation commit to the development of a range of skills essential for their overall competence. One set of skills focuses on teaming, including the ability to design and facilitate a meeting that produces meaningful results, and the ability to form and facilitate a team. The skills development also includes interpersonal relations skills such as coaching, counseling, and conflict resolution. A second set of skills is in the business arena— knowing how the business makes money, how it meets customer needs, how the organization works, and how the production functions function. A third set of skills is in specific technical areas, including computing and networking. Cross-training creates bench depth so that meeting customer needs are not dependent on specific individuals. Finally, a percentage of the workforce has change management skills, which involve knowledge of how organizations, teams, and individuals change over time, and how to initiate and manage a change process.

3. *Learning behavior.* Learning processes are created based on a commitment to increase speed and effectiveness for the customer by learning from successes and mistakes. Starting with a commitment from leadership, specific learning tools, methods, and processes are integrated into all organizational processes.

Business Processes

There are two sets of business processes that enable the relationship-based corporation to realize speed and effectiveness: external and internal.

- *External processes.* As discussed earlier, the company can ensure that it is meeting the ongoing needs of its customers and suppliers by creating partnerships that involve formalized agreements for how those needs will be met. These agreements clarify roles, processes, and expectations.
- *Internal processes.* Internally, teams and groups working on meeting customer needs will be cross-functional. Work processes are streamlined, duplication eliminated, and new technologies introduced that add value, increase speed, and enhance quality. Centers of excellence within the business are created to capitalize on the intellectual capital of its members, wherever it may reside.

A Team-Based Structure

There is an old saying that form follows function. In a relationship-based corporation, both are predicated on being aligned with the core values of the business—that is, that form follows function follows values. Because those core values are trust and respect as well as speed, the organizational structure is flat and flexible. Teams provide a way to organize the actions and behaviors of the workforce to ensure internal alignment and the most effective use of resources. But a critical distinction exists between a company that uses teams from time to time and a company that is team-based. The relationship-based corporation is 100 percent team-based. Everyone is on a "home team"—and only one home team—to ensure that team gridlock does not occur. People can move to another home team depending on where they are needed and may also serve on project teams as needed.

The structure is flat and networked. As suggested by Figure 4-2, there is usually no need to have more than three levels in

Figure 4-2. The structure of a relationship-based corporation.

the business: the strategic leadership team, business unit teams, and support partner teams.

•   *The strategic leadership team.* The strategic leadership team provides overall direction to the business, sets goals and objectives to meet customer and shareholder expectations, forms alliances and joint ventures, and ensures the overall performance of the business.

•   *Business unit teams.* Business units are the front line of the relationship-based corporation. They may be organized by product line, a combination of products, customer, or geography.

Their focus is on building strong partnerships with each customer, usually formal relationships, that spell out the processes by which the customers get their needs met. Business unit teams also produce the product or service, deliver it, and ensure its quality and value. Each business unit has a management team that focuses on implementation of the business plan. To ensure internal alignment, integration of strategy, customer requirements, and speedy implementation, membership of the business unit management team is expanded to include some members of the strategic leadership and support partner teams.

• *Support partner teams.* The more traditional functions of human resources, finance, marketing, logistics, maintenance, engineering, and information services work cross-functionally to meet the needs of the business units. No longer siloed, each business unit team has members with specialized knowledge in each of these areas. Everyone is focused on ensuring that the business unit teams have what they need to be successful, and are measured accordingly.

In this flat structure, there is no hierarchy of teams, since power is not the driver. Instead, the customer is. Walls between departments eventually disappear as teams work across functions to meet customer needs. There are no titles to speak of since upward mobility is no longer the goal. Financial incentives for high performance, innovation, and value-added work may be found in team-based rewards, corporation-wide bonuses, or benefits programs. Nonfinancial rewards become very important, including professional development, increased responsibility, project management opportunities, and travel. Measurement of individual and team performance comes from the customer, leadership, and fellow team members.

Corporate Outcomes: Trust, Speed, and Integrity

In any business, outcomes are typically of three types—those that reflect the character of the relationships inside the business, those that represent bottom-line results, and those that characterize its reputation. These outcomes reflect how well the covenant has worked and how effectively the membership has addressed strategic, customer, and implementation challenges of the business.

1. *Relationship outcomes—Trust.* The quality and character of workplace relationships, as well as customer relationships, are transformed from fear-based competition to trust-based collaboration. Because the culture of the workplace is based on the principles of trust and mutual respect, the focus of relationships is on honest, authentic dialogue rather than on hidden agendas and being right. Work is based on creating win-win situations. While members of the workforce will take some time migrating toward a high level of trust in their teams, the focus is on building new bridges. With no need to climb ladders, the intellectual capital and energy of the workforce is focused on one thing—exceeding the expectations of the customer. Where there have been broken relationships, the focus is on healing the past and learning new ways to work together.

2. *Bottom-line results—Speed.* Business results are produced at significantly higher rates of speed. With internal conflict at a minimum and trust increasing all the time, the workforce is more focused on the customer's needs, efficient production, creating new ways to meet their needs, and quality. With increased communications, dialogue, and internal alignment on what matters, the workforce is more willing to be flexible and adapt. Labor disputes all but disappear. Business processes are easily simplified since no one has any turf to protect. Manufacturing processes and service delivery systems are speeded up, new technologies are more easily introduced, inventory turns are increased, and production errors are reduced. As a result, financial results continue to improve, as does shareholder value.

3. *Reputational outcomes—Integrity.* The relationship-based corporation creates a reputation of integrity and the highest standards of conduct. Corporate decisions are made only after looking at the options through the lens of values, mission, and vision of the company as well as its carefully crafted code of ethics. Everyone in the company is responsible for upholding

these ethics, and honor once again becomes a critical ingredient of professionalism.

In Closing

Our vision is to create a relationship-based corporation, a workplace that will be governed by the principles of trust and mutual respect, not power and fear. This workplace is one where relationships, not transactions, are a central concern. People are an end, not a means. In a relationship-based corporation, the focus is also on value, not cost; on mutual interest rather than individual gain; and, most importantly, on the customer rather than ego. As a result, trust, speed, and integrity are the logical outcomes.

Impossible? Utopia? Not at all. While this may be an ideal type, there are already companies, like MSI, that are operating in whole or in part in this manner. The framework described in this chapter presents what is possible. The question becomes whether or not it is our intent to evolve toward a more trust-based approach to work so that we can lead at the speed of change.

To evolve successfully, however, we must have a methodology that drives the change from the principles of trust and mutual respect. We must have a powerful framework that leverages the character and will of the workforce and provides a discipline for the journey. Understanding that methodology is our next milestone.

Let's be clear, however, that, from this point forward, our journey will take us into what for most companies will be uncharted territory. We will work to unlearn the past, become aware of our values and options, and then consciously choose to change. We will look in the mirror each morning to determine who has the responsibility for change. We will learn to give up the old paradigm so that we can realize our own potential as well as that of those around us. Given the results we can achieve, it is a journey worth taking.

PART TWO

Creating a Relationship-Based Corporation

5

//

Achieving Sustainable Change

"When change processes fail, it is usually due to a lack of character, will, or discipline."

//

"I want it to work," Trevor said to Sarah as they looked over their change strategy. "I want nothing more than to have MSI work at a high level of trust, be team-based, and be customer-driven. We know that is the best way to work. And I know we have to do this to increase speed, but sometimes, like today, it just does not feel like a risk worth taking." Trevor had just come from a meeting with the president and the senior management team. Warren was particularly disturbed that the change plan he asked to have enacted in nine months was now going to take over a year to finalize. He still did not understand the importance of front-loading the change process and making sure that the workforce understood the new direction before implementation. Trevor had been told to cut the ramp-up time to two months.

"I did not feel particularly courageous," Trevor continued, "going to the team and saying, 'We will get more speed and trust if you give up your title and control over your department so we can become flat, flexible, and fast.' Why should they want to do that?" Sarah tried to console him as best she could by putting the impending change in perspective. "I know that change is always risky, but frankly, Trevor, if we do nothing we

may soon all be out of a job. Our customer and employee satis-faction ratings have been dropping for three years now. Our market share is down 10 percent, and the future looks pretty grim because we cannot keep up with all the changes in the market. We have no choice but to try this approach.'' Sarah con-tinued, ''Now, do we have to become a relationship-based cor-poration? I think so. You and I both know that all of the other programs we have tried just backfired. We ended up worse off because of them.''

For most businesses today, the dance of rapid change is already in play. The question is whether they are prepared to participate. There is nothing romantic about change, taking risks, or trying to transform institutions that have been successful using a more traditional approach to work. It's downright scary. It can be pain-ful. And yet business leaders know their companies must change to remain competitive.

MSI learned, during the last twenty years of change experi-ments, that these initiatives failed, either because the commit-ment to change was unclear, the methodology was ineffective, or leadership lacked patience. Another way of saying this is that the change initiatives lacked the character, will, and/or disci-pline to succeed. There has to be a better way to initiate and sustain change in a way that enables a company to increase its internal trust levels, speed to market, and effectiveness in its work with customers.

The purpose of this chapter is to describe such a method for change, a way that enables businesses to transform themselves while building trust at the speed of change. First, we will look at four traditional approaches to change management that are widely used today to understand their underlying assumptions and their effectiveness in terms of sustainable change. We will identify the ten critical mistakes companies make in these change initiatives and the seven guidelines for success. Then, we will look at a fifth approach to sustainable change, the Col-laborative Method, and its three guiding principles that increase the probability of success—Character, Will, and Discipline. We will learn that to achieve sustainable change, the initiative must be driven by the integrity of the leadership, and ownership by the people who must live with the consequences. Vision, strategy, process, and structural changes are all integral parts of the methodology, but without the trust of the workforce and the integrity of leadership, it will not work. In the next chapter, we will look at the specific phases, steps, and tools involved in implementation.

Traditional Approaches to Change

Every change methodology is based on a set of assumptions about how a business can best transform itself and achieve sustainable competitive advantage. By employing this strategy, the goal for most businesses is to increase market share, lower costs, increase profitability, improve quality, and increase morale in the workforce. Most approaches adopted, however, have been on a single track. They focus on one dimension of the company or on one technique. Some approaches have claimed to be revolutionary techniques for radical transformation and cost cutting. Some have claimed to be focused on quality or empowerment. Some made no claims at all. But when all the dust has cleared, few if any of them have resulted in sustainable competitive advantage or change. In many instances, one method gave way to another, as companies chased after solutions. We will look at four standard change approaches which have been used: (1) vision- or strategy-based; (2) structure-first; (3) process-based; and (4) technology-driven. We will follow MSI on its journey using these methods, and then see what lessons we can learn.

Vision- or Strategy-Based Change

This was the first approach MSI tried. The premise of a vision- or strategy-based approach to change is that the direction for the change comes from the top. Warren hired a consultant to frame the strategy, took the senior management team on a retreat, and developed the strategic business vision for the company. A summary document laid out the new direction. Then it was communicated to the workforce by each department head, followed by a company-wide meeting that included a video presentation.

In some companies, in the spirit of fostering more participation, focus groups are used to solicit input, with a special emphasis on middle management and first-line supervisors. The fundamentals of the overall direction, however, are usually not negotiable. One critical key to success for this approach is that every member of the workforce be able to "see themselves" in the company's future vision. Without meaningful workforce involvement, visioning may be viewed as just another program.

For MSI, after the retreat, there was no noticeable change in behavior or results. There *was* renewed emphasis on beating the competition—but it did not happen. Without effective dialogue, there was no ownership; it was just another failed initiative. The workforce must be involved in the design of the strategy if they are expected to implement it. They would do the work, but the message they would hear is that they did not matter. Building trust is not a desired outcome of this approach. Sustainable change typically does not happen with a vision- or strategy-based approach.

Structure-First Change

When the vision approach did not work at MSI, senior management decided to try to meet market pressures by restructuring the business. They decentralized along product lines, forming five strategic business units. They consolidated the shared service organizations—human resources, finance, and marketing—and decided to outsource information systems. The premise behind this structure-first approach to change was that centralized control could quickly streamline the organization, the workforce would support it, and the company could create speed and competitive advantage. It could be done quickly, and there was a belief that the behavior of the workforce would automatically change as a result.

Reorganizations are sometimes used to avoid dealing with difficult people or situations. They can be used to improve competitive position or help the company build alliances, partnerships, or joint ventures, or to merge with another company. In most structural change processes, however, positions are eliminated, people are fired or moved into new positions, new organizational relationships are established, new functions are assigned, and resources are reallocated. But the real success of a structural change hinges on whether there is cultural acceptance by the people affected by the change.

Typically, the workforce is not involved, which means employees are less likely to accept the changes. Implementation, however, usually proceeds anyway, just without a lot of enthusiasm. Without involvement, people coming from different departments, cultures, or belief systems do not have a common ground upon which to stand. In the months of dislocation that follow a structural change, they work hard at not rocking the boat and focus on getting tasks done; that is, they are transaction based. But at some point, usually shortly after the change process starts, the honeymoon is over, conflicts emerge, and even just concentrating on the tasks at hand simply does not work anymore. Major conflicts, irritations, frustrations, and even resentments set in as people harden their positions, not out of malice but because there is no alternative way to build trust. Structure-first programs do not result in sustainable change.

Process-Based Change

There are at least three types of process-based change—two that focus on people and one that involves business processes. MSI tried all three.

1. *The awareness approach.* The premise behind awareness or communications approaches to change is the belief that, with the right information, the workforce will make the right decision to back the initiative and will alter its behavior accordingly. Typically, knowledge does not translate into new behavior for many people, and there is little assurance that the communication of information to people results in buy-in. MSI leadership embarked on a six-week market and customer awareness program to create a shared view of the problems the business faced and how to deal with them. Workshops, speakers, symposia, tapes, and newsletters were the order of the day. But while the

workforce appreciated the investment the company was making in its education, employees were more interested in seeing fundamental changes in behavior and a realignment of the power relationship. At MSI, this cognitive approach produced some initial enthusiasm and energy, but within weeks that energy had dissipated. Nothing had really changed at MSI.

2. *The experiential approach.* The premise behind experiential or learning approaches to change is that if we give people opportunities to see their behavior and the effects it has on others, or if they have the opportunity to learn new skills, they will change their way of working. Some do. Most do not. The MSI team tried this approach to change as well. Each department identified its branch groups as teams. In its existing teams, the workforce went through two weeks of team training for the purpose of increasing awareness of how employees worked in groups and to increase synergy. They experienced both indoor group work and outdoor ropes courses. The belief in using this approach was that, if everyone went through the same value-based training, somehow, by osmosis, they would transfer the individual value of their experiences to the workplace, and a critical mass of shared values would be created. What happened at MSI was that the process was stereotyped as "team games" and "touchy-feely stuff." Everyone was more involved, but there was virtually no significant impact on the workplace or the culture. Typically, it is very difficult to achieve sustainable, organization-wide change through training or experiential approaches. There are different levels of ownership and buy-in, and often people feel the process is being done to them rather than with them.

3. *A business process approach.* The third type of change MSI used was to change business processes, using total quality and reengineering. MSI tried Total Quality Management (TQM) because of its need to shift the focus of work processes to the customer, to improve quality, and to simplify business processes. The result was supposed to be a commitment to continuous improvement, greater efficiency, and therefore higher levels of customer satisfaction. The MSI workforce went to TQM training, learned the steps in the process, and established measures for performance. Their teams kept getting stuck on their

inability to reach true consensus on the root causes of their quality issues and breakdowns in their interpersonal relationships. There was belief that the real solutions had already been determined elsewhere. Within six months, TQM became just another program. The plaques on the walls remained, but the commitment to this change did not last.

Undaunted by the failures and still driven by the need for speed, the MSI leadership then decided to reengineer critical business processes. Here, the premise was that if overlap and duplication could be eliminated and processes streamlined, a "revolution" would occur in the structure and performance of the business. With an attitude of "No more Mr. Nice Guy," MSI hired a consulting company to take out 25 percent of the cost. This translated into a significant loss of jobs. For four months, consultants lived at MSI, going over every system, mapping every process, and looking at how to reduce head count. The objective was to turn the company on its head and totally reevaluate what work really needed to be done. It was an attractive concept, but when implemented at MSI, the result was a very expensive downsizing, as well as resistance from the rest of the workforce. The people who remained ended up with more work, and MSI had to hire back many of the laid-off experts as consultants because it had lost its capability to deliver. Costs went up, satisfaction went down, and resentment in the workforce lingered.

For many companies, one result of reengineering has been the breaking of the traditional psychological contract with the workforce. Reengineering does not believe that the workforce should "own" the change, because that would be a conflict of interest. Middle management is seen as the greatest resister to change and must be reassigned or laid off. The belief is that only objective outsiders can create the reductions in head count or process changes needed to truly revolutionize the business. While many mature businesses *do* need to refocus their business on the customer and simplify processes that have become nonproductive, the failure to involve the workforce in meaningful decision making about how best to realign the business processes has resulted in a broken covenant. Trust is usually not on the radar screen.

Technology-Driven Change

Tied closely to the reengineering phenomenon is a strongly held view that information technology solutions should drive the change process in a business. There is a belief that competitive, global, and network issues can be resolved with the introduction of new technologies—for the supply chain, customer relations, marketing, collaboration inside the business, and networking. As companies have moved from mainframes to distributed and networked computing systems, and as supply-chain management has become essential to increasing speed to market, information technology solutions have become a central driver for organizational change. The premise is that people need information to be processed and shared so that decisions can be made quickly. It follows, then, that the installation of technology-based information solutions should meet that need.

At MSI, this meant that a systems integration technology company was hired to install a new computing platform using a new set of software modules that covered all their functions. Not only was the workforce expected to embrace the new system, but it would have to be retrained to use it. Many older employees were either unwilling or unable to change, and were retired early. But what was not understood was that the introduction of new technologies involves a lot more than installing equipment and learning new software.

For most people, new technologies represent a significant culture change in how they work. They often have to change their habits, standards, and even people they work with. They may end up working with new people when before they were alone, or working alone when they used to be in a group. They most likely will have to give up the ways they have successfully worked for years and learn new, more complex, and sometimes incomplete systems. Often the new software is insufficiently tailored to meet their needs, and methods that had seemed perfectly efficient before are replaced with cumbersome, expensive, and difficult ones. Typically, the workforce is not involved in the decision to initiate this change, hire the consultants, or adopt the solution. As a result, without dialogue and involvement, the new technology may not be used to its optimum. This approach relies on power, creates resistance, costs a lot of money, often slows down the business by diverting energy and resources from other priorities, and usually does not produce trust or sustainable change.

Ten Mistakes Companies Make in Implementing Change

What we saw MSI do was commit most of the mistakes companies make in trying to do the right thing—not because its leaders willfully tried to fail or hurt people, but because they had never been on this journey before and they relied upon their best knowledge at the time to get the job done. The values, mindsets, and biases of the leadership drive change initiatives. But the mistakes are legend and have been repeated at many companies. What did MSI learn? The leadership seemed to fall into the following ten categories.

1. *It's about control, not change.* There are many business leaders who talk about change, but when they believe it will affect their control of the business, the change process stops. They may become critical of the team process or consensus decision making, say it's taking too long, or that it is becoming too expensive. At the heart of the concern is a perceived loss of power and control.

2. *The search for the silver bullet.* Change is usually treated as a project that has a beginning, middle, and end. It is a destination. It is about some issue or problem in the business that needs to be fixed, rather than behavior, attitudes, beliefs, or the corporate culture. So the solution is a program-of-the-month approach, which will yield a magic solution or a quick fix. There is little or no recognition that lasting change involves the entire organizational system.

3. *When in doubt, restructure.* There is a tendency to take the easy way out in an effort to orchestrate a significant change. It is a lot easier to reorganize, decentralize, or outsource a func-

tion than it is to build ownership, change behavior, or install team-based systems, even though the outcomes of structural approaches are predictable.

4. *Been there, done that.* Cynicism, skepticism, and the NIH (not invented here) syndrome play a major role in the failure of change initiatives. We have become jaded by all the failed promises. We have tried all the programs. We have had it done to us or for us by outsiders, and none of it worked. There is no reason to believe that this next program will be any different.

5. *No ownership.* One of the reasons for this cynicism, as well as change failure, is the lack of authentic and appropriate involvement. It is much easier to have an outside consulting firm do the work for the company, or to create a change team and have it drive the process. Full involvement takes time, money, and organization. But without full involvement at the appropriate level, those responsible for implementing the change will feel little or no ownership of it, will feel distrusted, and will not have a high level of commitment to its effective execution.

6. *Not managing expectations.* Change is about hope. Change is about realizing dreams. Change is about fixing the things that have been driving us crazy about our jobs. And since an upset is an unfulfilled expectation, most change efforts fail in part because leadership does not find out what the expectations of the workforce are and/or does not manage them effectively.

7. *Impatience.* Because change initiatives are about control, quick fixes, and point solutions rather than fundamental behavioral or cultural changes, business leaders get impatient if there are no demonstrable results within ninety days. The notion that these changes take years in large companies, or that change is a journey, runs contrary to the way in which we believe we must run businesses today. Even with the promise of speed, higher morale, and greater creativity, the results are not tangible or quick enough for many business leaders.

8. *It's always something.* Adding to the impatience is the rate of change in market conditions, turnover rates, new technologies, competitor challenges, budget reductions, leadership changes, or nonperforming projects. In any given twelve-month

period for a change initiative, there will be a number of major business changes, any one of which can derail the process.

9. *Default to the negative.* One of the more interesting phenomena causing change failures is the apparent tendency we have to assume the worst about others, to believe that no matter what positive forces are at work, sooner or later it will go bad. In many instances, the cynicism is justified. People have been disappointed so many times, they expect the change effort to be dropped or modified. Even when leadership speaks its commitment, distrust is high.

10. *We don't know how.* In most instances, companies have not yet learned how to implement a system change, or do not know how to change the culture. Because resources have been so heavily invested in structure-first, technology, or process-based changes, there has been little emphasis on the powerful role that culture and behavior play in enabling sustainable change.

Seven Guidelines for Successful Change Management

These reasons for change failure point to the clear need for a new approach to sustainable change, especially if we expect to build trust at the speed of change and to evolve a corporation from a transaction-based approach to work to one based on relationships. Here are seven guidelines for sustainable change to help us develop this new methodology.

Guideline 1: Organizations do not cause change—people do. People make conscious choices about their values, how they behave, whether or not to alter the ways they work, and whether or not to effect changes in an organization's structure, processes, culture, or systems.

Guideline 2: Change is evolutionary, not revolutionary. Because the market demands speed while people are slow to change, organizational change is evolutionary and not revolutionary. We've already tried the revolutionary approach (reengineering), and it backfired. People need time to understand why they must change, to own it, and then choose to alter their behavior. They cannot be forced to do so, and attempts at force will only result in long-term distrust, resistance, and lowered productivity.

Guideline 3: People take care of what they own. Typically people do not wash rented cars. To value the change, they must understand it, have value for it, and see how the change will benefit them. If they own the change, they will implement it effectively.

The Strategic Alliance

Two Fortune 100 companies sought to create a strategic alliance that would result in the investment of $500 million within nine months in a series of properties. The legal, financial, and structural arrangements had taken thirteen months to complete. Within three weeks of signature, the "alliance" began to falter due to fundamental cultural, behavioral, and management differences, particularly between two senior officers, one in each company. An assessment discovered that the top leaders in both companies gave the alliance three to six months to live.

   The collaborative method was applied by engaging the top business leaders of both companies in an alliance-building process that focused on their common financial goals and business objectives, and what it was going to take to get them there. Within three weeks, a commitment by the CEOs of both companies was made to create a collaborative, trust-based alliance led by a senior management team from both organizations. Within six weeks after that, the team had invested $150 million, with the help of off-line coaching and a structured cross-company teaming process. Within nine months, more than $575 million had been invested. The cycle time for the completion of the management contracts governing the deals was reduced from one year to two weeks. Within three years, the Alliance had invested close to $2 billion, and it was institutionalized at the Executive Committee level of both companies.

Guideline 4: Change involves the entire system. Organizations are living organisms. A change in one part of the corporate body affects every other part of the organization. Sustainable change requires a holistic perspective, which looks at every part of the organizational system. The change methodology must be able to do this.

Guideline 5: Sustainable change is culture driven. Sustainable change is about driving the change from the fundamentals of principle, shared values, and new behaviors/actions based on a foundation of trust, respect, and integrity. It is about the character, will, and discipline of leadership teams and groups to make the changes necessary to meet the need for speed.

Guideline 6: Sustainable change comes from the inside out. Lasting change comes from the inside out of each person, each team, and each group. This change is manifested in behavior showing responsibility for the change, actions which implement the change, positive attitudes, and a willingness to grow.

Guideline 7: It is a journey that requires character, will, and discipline. Because sustainable change is a journey and not a program, it will involve some level of struggle as we work to redefine who we are and how we truly want to work together across an entire organization. This will mean commitment, competence, and the will to stay the course, especially in times of adversity and ambiguity.

So how do we increase our prospects for success in changing our organizations and the way we work? In applying these seven guidelines, we can evolve into a relationship-based corporation over time. But it will require a commitment to start from the inside out, from the top of the organization, and to involve the entire workforce. It will require us to use a systems-oriented methodology, which builds from the beliefs, values, and behaviors of members of the organization. Everyone must get involved in the journey at some level to own the change, align with the strategy, and help implement the new direction. Energy is then focused on trust, not transactions.

Culture-Driven Change:
The Collaborative Method*

We have to go faster to keep up with the market, and slower if we really want to get there. It is the central paradox of change management. The more we drive change from the top, the less buy-in we get. The more we try point solutions to increase speed, the more complex the problems seem to become. The more training we do to become teams, the less change we seem to get. In spite of our positive intent, we seem to have missed the most critical driver for a change process—the culture of the workplace. This means the beliefs and values of the people in the workforce, their inherent need for trust and respect, their desire for meaningful work relationships, and their energy and commitment to win.

As we build a change methodology that will enable us to create and sustain a relationship-based corporation, we need to remember that how a change process starts is usually how it ends up. If it starts with a focus on control, it will end up as a controlling change process. So we cannot expect an organization to evolve into a relationship-based corporation by employing any methodology other than one based on a set of principles central to building trust-based relationships. Similarly, if the change methodology is solely focused on preventing the mistakes of the past, we may end up falling victim to a methodology that is a patchwork quilt of point solutions.

Earlier in this chapter, we reviewed four standard approaches to business transformation and found that they were unable to realize sustainable change. Now let's look more closely at a fifth approach, which I call *culture-first change*, or the Collaborative Method. This is a method that harnesses the power of the workplace culture to the process of changing an organization, department, or even a team. It enables us to evolve

---

*This methodology was first described in the author's previous book, *Transforming the Way We Work: The Power of the Collaborative Workplace* (New York: AMACOM, 1995). In this section, the methodology is significantly upgraded to reflect advancements in the implementation of large-scale change processes developed in more than a hundred change projects since that time.

from having a transaction-based workplace to a relationship-based workplace by building from the inside out, and by building on the three core principles of successful change management: Character, Will, and Discipline. By building on the character of leadership and the will of an organization's workforce, the company can, with discipline, gradually evolve from a culture of power, control, and fear to a culture of relationships, mutual respect, and trust. As we shall see, however, it is not an easy journey, but is really the only journey that will enable us to achieve the speed and flexibility needed to compete in the information age.

The Collaborative Method involves building trust-based relationships, ownership, and alignment across the entire organization. As a systems approach, collaborative change produces high energy in individuals and synergy among teams. This is accomplished through high involvement and by ensuring that everyone understands the direction in which the business is moving. With greater trust and ownership comes greater willingness to be responsible and accountable for the business. With that comes greater flexibility, adaptability to change, speed, and customer focus. The interlocking circles in Figure 5-1 show how these core principles are integrated. One cannot work without the others, and at key junctures in the change process, these principles overlap.

The Character Principle

The *Character* of this methodology involves the values, principles, and beliefs about the type of organization that will be created, the nature of the covenant between leadership and the workforce, the role of the business itself, and the way in which the change process itself will be conducted. It may be defined in three arenas: people, business, and the change process itself.

• *People values.* To become a relationship-based corporation, this method places the highest value on the needs and hopes of the leadership and the workforce. It focuses on their covenant with each other and their responsibilities for the success of the change process. The core values include building mu-

Figure 5-1. The collaborative method of change.

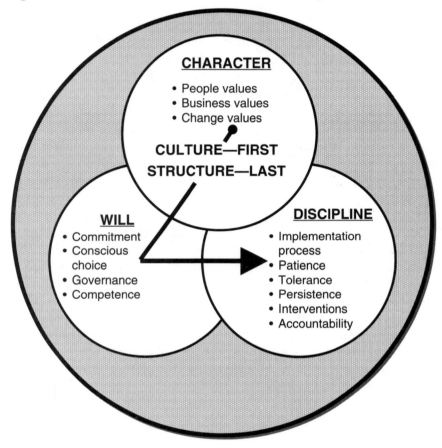

tual trust and respect as well as ownership for the change process and the business. Equally important is ensuring strategic alignment across the business and maintaining a high level of integrity in the conduct of work relationships.

• *Business values.* In the conduct of the business, this methodology places a high value on the needs of the market and customer base in setting the strategic direction of the business. There is recognition by all involved that cultural change inside the company is critical to meeting these needs on a continuing basis. There is also recognition that organizational changes will enable the business to achieve the speed and effectiveness customers need.

• *Change values*. In the conduct of the change process itself, this methodology recognizes that there must be a compelling need for the leadership and workforce to be willing to change, and that this need varies from company to company. It assumes the principle of evolutionary change, a comprehensive systems approach, and a commitment to keeping the process open. There is belief that sustainable change happens when it is part of real work. Real work in real time becomes a standard for success.

When combined, these values become a powerful foundation for driving the implementation of any change process, whether it is a project team or a large-scale introduction of a new technology, a merger, or a reorganization.

The Will Principle

The *Will* of this change methodology involves the ability to engage individuals and groups in making conscious choices about the future, to create a framework for change that causes them to act in a manner that is consistent with the principles of trust and relationship. It involves individual and group capacity to change, the competencies to implement their intention, and the willingness to act in a way that brings honor to the change. The will of an individual, team, or company to change, for example, means that when the next program of the month comes along, it is evaluated in the context of the principles, vision, and intent of the change process. It is not automatically adopted and the previous effort suspended. Conscious choices are made to honor the direction chosen. The will of the company is about its determination to achieve its goals. There is a plan, a strategy, and a commitment to see it through to completion. There are four arenas where the will is essential, as follows.

• *A commitment to the journey*. Commitment means more than words. It means actions, resources, and follow-through. It means an uncommon pledge of one's integrity to oneself and others to see the change through. In the early stages of a change initiative, be it large or small, leadership makes a firm commitment to take the journey and then to see it through to its successful completion. Similarly, each individual in the company must make some level of commitment to the change based on his or her understanding of the need and ownership of the process. For all concerned, this means full participation and taking responsibility for the success of the effort.

• *Conscious choices along the way.* Conscious choice requires the individual to take full responsibility for the decision being made. In this methodology, it means people are aware of the options and their consequences at various points along the way, and make decisions for which they are willing to be held accountable. There is no room for finger pointing or shifting responsibility to others.

• *Putting a governance framework in place.* To ensure consistency in the implementation of the change process, a common template is used to front-load each step of the journey. Whether it is for a team, group, department, or entire organization, this governance process ensures that the core values of the process are in place, especially ownership and alignment. Expectations are managed as shared perceptions are created. In so doing, integrity is brought to the initiative.

• *Building the competence for change.* To ensure the effectiveness and sustain ability of the change process, there must be competency in various types of skill sets—in orchestrating a change process, team development, meeting design and management, interpersonal relations, change interventions, and organizational psychology. The objective of this methodology is to build a fairly high level of self-sufficiency so that the workforce can self-resource its ongoing change efforts.

With the character of the change process having a solid, value-based foundation, the leadership and workforce are in a position to demonstrate their will to accomplish that change. Actions, however, must follow words. Behaviors must reflect the new character of the business. It takes strength, courage, and the conviction of one's beliefs to ensure the success of any change effort—that is, Discipline. It is far too easy to backslide, rationalize, give up, or slide by.

The Discipline Principle

While the Will expresses the commitment, *Discipline* implements it during the journey. Discipline involves patience, tolerance for ambiguity and adversity, reassurance that we are on the right course, and the ability to hold people's feet to the fire when they get uncomfortable. The discipline of a change methodology involves creating a system of governance that ensures that commitments are honored, skills are built, and people are held accountable. This means that when there is internal resistance, reversion to old control-based behaviors, or the desire to quit the process, there are processes in place to intervene and to call the organization to account to honor their commitments.

In the Collaborative Method, Discipline is about implementation of the change process; but more importantly, it is about how the company handles risk, fear of failure, the challenge of real change, and their patience in seeing that change through to the next phase of the journey. There are four essential elements here.

1. *The processes of implementation.* There are many implementation processes and steps that must be managed, and in the Collaborative Method, while there is a leadership process for the management of change, successful implementation is everyone's responsibility. Implementation is team-based, with clear roles and responsibilities, including planning, communications, decision making, problem-solving, team development, and skills training. It is a proactive set of processes—anticipating, involving, aligning, organizing, dialoguing, assessing, and learning. This is a dynamic set of processes involving many people, their needs, concerns, hopes, and expectations. These processes are based on the recognition that change by its very nature increases anxiety. The method will, therefore, constantly evolve.

2. *Patience, tolerance, and persistence.* There seems to be an internal clock in our systems that is ready to move on to the

next program, technique, or hoped-for solution within ninety days. We are an impatient people. We also expect change processes to run smoothly, without conflicts or ups and downs, and to achieve the desired results right on schedule. Not so with human behavior, organizational behavior, or the dynamics of significant change, let alone the evolution of a corporation's way of working. The Collaborative Method's Discipline requires internal self-control in the face of expected breakdowns in the process, or the realities of people confronting old ways of doing things and trying to change their behavior. This discipline requires commitment even through total, outright failure on the first, second, or third try. The Collaborative Method's Discipline also requires persistence in the face of external adversity—a drop in share price, turnover of key players, a need to reduce costs, or other significant events. Without patience, tolerance, and persistence, there can be no integrity on the journey.

3. *Effective interventions.* Even with persistence, the discipline of this method involves strategically timed interventions to ensure that as few land mines as possible explode. This means managing expectations, resolving conflicts, building value at every step, ensuring the effective management of the process, anticipating breakdowns, putting preventions in place, and calling on the entire organization to honor its commitments. It is the critical task of those responsible for interventions to put the integrity of the leadership and workforce on the line.

4. *Accountability for results.* No change process can be successful unless specific results are achieved. The discipline of this method involves identification of short, medium, and long-range results that will generate confidence in the process, in the people, and in the business. While everyone is ultimately accountable for producing results, the orchestration of key milestones, celebrations of those successes, and learning from the experience are important in building momentum. The discipline of this method also means that, should results not be realized, there is a calling to account of the key stakeholders to understand why. This process is a check to ensure that the process is kept in balance with actual results produced. In exercising the discipline of this method, each member of the organization has

the opportunity to become a disciple, to be a teacher of others, and a catalyst for the change journey. By "teaching the walk," critical mass is achieved—that is, that point at which the change becomes self-sustaining, and takes on a life of its own. When critical mass is achieved, the change journey ceases to be a risk, but it becomes a challenge to grow.

Culture-First, Structure-Last

Now we come to the arrow in Figure 5-1, "culture-first, structure-last." The Collaborative Method, with its emphasis on core values as the driver of the change process, is by definition a culture-first approach to organizational change because it puts core values ahead of strategy, structure, process, or technology. Each of those elements comes into play in due course, but only after leadership and the workforce have together taken ownership of the initiative. When people in a business take responsibility for the decisions they make to change how they work together, when they align on the core values of trust, respect, and integrity, and take ownership of the change process, they are implementing a culture-first approach that is collaborative, relationship-based, and truly transformative.

With their character, will, and discipline on the line, behaviors begin to change, work relationships and business processes begin to improve significantly, and over time the entire way in which the business functions is transformed. Because the workforce naturally wants to have a trust-based workplace, the culture-driven approach to change releases and then harnesses their energy for fundamental, sustainable change.

In Closing

When both leadership and the workforce realize that trust-based, collaborative change is truly within their grasp, that it is theirs to create or to lose, their focus on the customer, quality, creativity, productivity, and profitability takes on a whole new meaning. For now the change is theirs. This began to happen at

MSI when Trevor turned to Sarah, after reviewing the methodology for change, and said, "We tried everything else, and they did not work for us. What we learned, though, was that without ownership, without trust, and without integrity in our approach to change, we will never achieve our goals. This really feels like it will work. The values are on target, there is more involvement than I think we know how to deal with, but when all is said and done, there won't be anyone at MSI who can say that he or she did not have a chance to be responsible for the change."

Then, ever the skeptic, Trevor added, "But the devil is in the details." Trevor is right. Only when the implementation of the methodology is successful will the true value and power of the Collaborative Method be realized. In our next chapter, the major phases of the implementation process are described, and then we will look at how the character, will, and discipline of the change process can be realized at all levels of a business.

6

//

Implementing the Collaborative Method

"Successful implementation is based on principle."

//

"Our integrity is on the line here as never before," Trevor said as he opened the meeting. He wanted the MSI senior management team to focus on the realities of their past, as well as what they had agreed to implement. The team had just decided to use the collaborative approach to change and was now working on the specifics of the implementation process. Warren, the president, acknowledged that Trevor was right—the devil was in the details. Without a solid implementation framework as a reference point, all the commitment in the world to become a relationship-based corporation would not matter.

Trevor and Sarah pointed out that the Collaborative Method's framework provided some degree of protection against failure. Certainly by increasing ownership and alignment in the change process, the shift would be from compliance to more collaboration. But what they emphasized most was the importance of the three principles for successful change we have just discussed—Character, Will, and Discipline. After all the change initiatives MSI had experienced, this time failure was not an option. So they were looking to this methodology and themselves to ensure their success.

///

Transforming a company's culture from transactions and compliance to one of relationships and collaboration is indeed a daunting challenge. Revolutionary approaches, we have seen, do not achieve sustainable change. People, and the organizations they work in, need time to understand, absorb, and integrate these changes into their daily work lives. By definition, change for individuals and organizations is evolutionary. It is best implemented in bite-sized chunks—a project, a customer, or a department at a time.

Implementation will also be more effective if change projects address a high-value business need, are focused on real work, and have measurable outcomes. Then, like a pebble thrown into a pond, when the first project is successful, there will be ripples of change across the organization. Then another project "pebble" can be thrown, and another until, within a relatively short period of time, the ripples overlap and a wave of change begins that eventually reaches across the entire business. How and when the pebbles are tossed requires skillful application of the change methodology. It is critical that the implementation be carefully orchestrated and implemented in accordance with the principles of character, will, and discipline. Implementing the Collaborative Method's approach to change involves five phases, which, if carefully orchestrated, enable a transaction-based corporation to evolve over time into a relationship-based workplace (see Figure 6-1).

Our purpose in this chapter is to describe each of the phases of a collaborative approach to implementation. These phases have been identified and developed as the result of many applications of this methodology in change processes large and small. They are, however, intended only to suggest a general road map, which I hope can be useful to a business in search of change. Within each phase, specific steps, tools, and processes are suggested to help you realize your goals. In the chapters to follow we will look at more specific applications of the methodology in terms of the leadership, workforce, and organizational changes needed to ensure success.

Phase I. Front-Loading the Process

How we begin a change process is often how it ends up. For the change process to achieve sustainable change, the collaborative

Figure 6-1. Implementing the collaborative method.

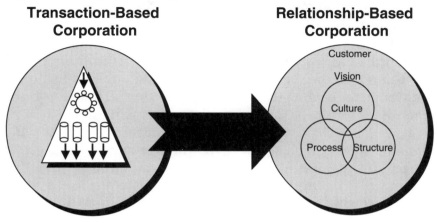

Phase I: Front-loading the process

Phase II: Initiating the change

Phase III: Building value

Phase IV: Achieving critical mass

Phase V: Sustaining the change

approach emphasizes front loading—that is, planning, building ownership, and ensuring alignment across the organization. We always seem to have time to do rework on a project, but never have the time to plan it properly on the front end. Then we wonder why our change processes become the program-of-the-month. The Character, Will, and Discipline of a change initiative that will transform an entire organization needs to be established at the beginning of the process. If there is hesitancy, timidity, or a lack of commitment to the actions necessary to implement the change, the initiative will founder rather quickly. It is better to not start at all than to begin with hesitation.

There is always concern at the beginning of a change process. That is normal. People have a right to ask whether the view is worth the climb. These concerns about the journey and the potential benefits or outcomes need to be fully aired. It may be that there is also a level of "not knowing" about the change process that goes beyond normal anxiety. We may not know precisely which step will follow the preceding one. That is also normal, and generally does not become an issue of principle. Most change efforts fail when the leadership intellectually agrees with the direction, but then turns its back or reverts to old behaviors when the going gets difficult. That result *is* a matter of principle.

Central to the success of this phase, then, is establishing of the Character of the process—that is, getting alignment on the core values for the process, obtaining agreement on the compelling need for change, getting the commitments needed, and planning how the change will be implemented. The greatest danger any business faces is rushing into an initiative like this without first doing the pre-work. Many business leaders think they know what the problem and the fix is. Impatient for results, they may insist on a particular approach or program, and wonder later why the change effort failed.

We can learn from NASA's emphasis on front-loading. When NASA engineers decide to send a shuttle into orbit, they allow approximately six to eight months of planning before the launch. They can abort lift-off even up to the last seconds. After lift-off, it takes the shuttle all of twelve minutes to reach orbit. Assuming that six months, conservatively, is spent in planning, this means that more than 99 percent of the time is invested in front-end planning. When our business missions are critical enough, or our survival depends on them, we need to do the proper front-loading. Just "doing it" will not produce quality results.

Because the evolution process is so critical to a company's ability to build trust at the speed of change, there are seven steps involved in front-loading the change process (see Figure 6-2).

Step 1: The compelling business need for change. Every successful change initiative begins with a compelling business need for change, not unlike MSI's competitive threats. This business need must be of such significance that it is accepted by all members as critical to the business. For example, it could involve the company's stock price, financial standing, or a key customer. The business need must be strategic and of long-range importance. Simply wanting to become more relationship-based and

Figure 6-2. Phase I: Front-loading the process.

Step 1:	Compelling business need for change.
Step 2:	Gain the commitment for action.
Step 3:	Create a team governance structure.
Step 4:	Understand the psychology of change.
Step 5:	Create an environment for healing.
Step 6:	Build a constituency for change.
Step 7:	Develop the change plan.

trusting is not sufficient reason for most people to be willing to invest heavily in this change process.

Step 2: Gain the commitment for action. With the business case for change in hand, a company's leadership needs to make a commitment to the change process that will meet that challenge. It needs to be a conscious choice for a vision of the future, the need for a new approach to work, and the method to achieve it. This commitment needs to be at a very high level of consensus among the key players, meaning they have no reservations about being fully responsible for the success of the change process. Without that level of commitment, the initiative probably should not be launched.

Step 3: Create a team governance structure. Collaborative change processes are usually initiated by a leadership team, which in turn sponsors a team to lead or orchestrate the change process, as well as a range of other teams that will implement change projects. Together these teams represent an initial governance structure to guide the change process. To succeed, each team needs to have a senior management sponsor. The sponsor provides legitimacy for the effort, guidance, resources, and support. Each team needs clarity regarding its task, its deliverables, time frame, and any limitations that can affect its operations. Sponsors also clarify expectations for the team's performance. Unfulfilled expectations can undermine the team's credibility and effectiveness.

Something About Harry

At one oil company, a cross-functional team had been asked to integrate more than thirty software applications into one seamless system, which would function effectively across five departments. Some of these departments did not speak with one another. A seven-member team was formed and sponsored by three business leaders who felt it was time to stop the internal competition.

During the first week of the team's work, it went through the collaborative team formation process as part of its "front-loading" so that whatever issues existed among the seven members could be resolved. They got snagged on scheduling their work. It seems that their chief technologist, Harry, had a rather large farm that required his presence during harvest time, which was only four weeks away. Harry could not guarantee he would be around to help the team at that time. The delivery date for their first product was five weeks away, and Harry's expertise was essential.

After six hours of trying to deal with Harry's intransigence, the team learned that Harry's resistance had nothing to do with his harvest. It had to do with how he had been treated in the last three years by his boss. He felt that his technical expertise had been disrespected, that his work had been ignored, and that now was his opportunity to be heard. Once Harry had had an opportunity to speak his mind and be heard, he and the team decided to conduct their meetings at his ranch during harvest time. Their operating agreement became known as "The Harry Agreement."

The team not only met their deliverable on time, but Harry became a central leader in the integration process, and found $6 million a year in lost revenues due to a lack of communication across departments. The team's work made a significant contribution to the company's success for years to come by beginning the process of cross-departmental collaboration.

With the team sponsored, and its purpose and expectations clarified, its members then agree on how they will work together. The team formation process is front-loaded as the members develop a set of operating agreements. If done properly, old conflicts are resolved, rules are clarified, and a high level of trust is created. The result is increased speed and efficiency. Then the team develops its charter, which spells out its mission, standards of business conduct, critical success factors, and roles and responsibilities. To develop its mission and understand its strategic link to the rest of the business, the team identifies its key stakeholders and their interests. Then they develop a road map or plan for the completion of their work and a communications plan that ensures understanding across the business about the team's purpose and progress.

Step 4: Understand the psychology of change. No change process will be successful unless there is an up-front understanding of the psychological dynamics of organizational change and what it takes for a change process to succeed. We know people naturally resist change. We know that their expectations, fears, and concerns can result in attitudes or behaviors that can block the success of a change effort. Therefore, to be responsible, we need to create a process to address them. The responsibility of the team leading the change process is to understand how people, processes, and systems respond to perceived threats to the status quo. They need to understand how to build ownership and value, and how to manage workforce expectations, as well as how to orchestrate the change process.

One powerful tool for orchestrating change is to have a clear intention or vision for the process. This means that the overall reason, goal, and focus for the change can inspire the workforce to action. It is above politics and the short term.

Another powerful tool is the participation of as many members of the business as feasible, and to do so as quickly as possible. A third set of tools involves preventions and interventions taken to maintain equilibrium and discipline during the change process. "Preventions" are those actions that leadership or the change team takes to prevent breakdowns in the change process, build value, and put the process on a positive footing. High involvement, for example, is a prevention strategy. And those actions that leadership or the change team does to correct something that has gone wrong are called "interventions." For example, if the communication process does not work and resistance to change is building, the team intervenes to correct the situation and keep the change initiative on track.

Step 5: Create an environment for healing. Most businesses today have been through a long list of change initiatives, many of which have left some deep scars. Before any significant change work proceeds, it is important to create an environment where some healing of those wounds can take place. How a healing environment is created will vary from organization to organization, and situation to situation. But a first step is getting out of denial, and recognizing there is a need for healing. One way to begin the healing process is to open up a dialogue with the workforce about what has happened in the past. Telling the truth in this dialogue creates an opportunity for people to get their concerns out on the table. However, there can be no fear of retribution if there is to be an honest dialogue. By acknowledging the reality of the past, leadership can create a level of credibility that translates directly into legitimacy to the change process.

In some instances, the pain is years old or is between two departments or two people. These conflicts can be addressed either through direct intervention in private, or through the team process itself. But it is essential that these issues or grudges from the past be acknowledged and, if at all possible, resolved. In time, they should go away. Without a healing process consciously initiated, the effectiveness and even the integrity of the change initiative can suffer.

Step 6: Build a constituency for change. Every change project or process has a constituency of key stakeholders who have a vested interest in its success. In this step, they must be enlisted and educated about the value of the initiative, and buy in at a significant level before moving too far into the planning process. Building a constituency for change starts at the top of the corporation, with at least the executive level in alignment. Whether the change initiative focuses on the entire corporation or on a single project, the compelling business need discussed earlier is a unifying force for generating buy-in. Leadership develops buy-in by using a variety of processes such as direct communications opening up a dialogue about the need for change and identifying their individual hopes and concerns about the initiative. Failure to build an open, trusting environment can produce significant breakdowns at any number of points along the way.

Among a business's most important stakeholders is the middle level of management. In the early stages of a change process, their buy-in is essential. When the organization starts to flatten, the role and responsibilities of middle management can change dramatically. They may feel threatened or they may welcome the change and seek to lead. A lot depends on how the change process is positioned.

One way to involve them is not unlike MSI's approach. Trevor and Sarah facilitated a series of workshops, which over several months, explored the following:

- The compelling business need for change
- A current-state analysis of business practices, culture, work processes, leadership practices, and structures that were impacting their ability to compete
- A breakdown and root-cause analysis of core problems
- A future-state vision for the business and workplace

On the shop floor or front lines of the business, the constituency development process is one of building value and understanding among the workforce, rather than consensus. One useful tool for doing this is called a "roundtable," which is in essence a focus group. Organized as part of an ongoing dialogue with small groups of associates, ten to fifteen at a time, the roundtable is an open forum for the workforce to be heard. How these roundtables are administered is key to their success. They cannot and should not be used as another vehicle for talking at the workforce. They are a listening post. They are a way to build or rebuild credibility. Their results should be processed and acted upon as quickly as possible. If listened to on a regular basis—say quarterly—the workforce will provide leadership with an audit checklist of concerns and issues, as well as hopes and expectations. The roundtables become an excellent way to manage expectations and build relationships.

Getting alignment with external stakeholders, including

customers and suppliers, is equally important, particularly if it affects the delivery of goods and/or services, pricing, quality, or speed. Leadership needs to pay particularly close attention here so it can manage their expectations, listen to their concerns, and engage them in the change process. One particularly good way to do this is by creating formal partnerships, which enable them to have a regular dialogue around their mutual needs, concerns, and expectations. With the emphasis on building relationship and trust, the partnerships are put in place before the change occurs. If there are breakdowns during the change initiative, they will have a way to address their concerns without pulling their business.

Step 7: Develop the change plan. When Alice faced the Cheshire cat in Lewis Carroll's *Alice's Adventures in Wonderland* and asked which way she should go, the cat in effect responded by saying it depended on where she wanted to end up. If the future-state vision is to become a relationship-based workplace, the change plan must enable the business to get there. There are several key elements involved in the development of this change plan, some of which have been discussed earlier.

First, what is a change plan? At its most basic level, it is a map for the journey that shows you how to achieve your desired results. On another level, the change plan is the evidence of organizational alignment, a reflection of the shared values and understandings about where the people in the business have chosen to go. On still another level, it is a tactical and operational plan that shows exactly how the goals will be attained. This involves the core values driving the change plan, the leadership's intent and commitment to move in a new direction, and the specific ways in which the goals will be realized.

The development of any change plan must be tailored to the specific concerns and needs of the business. To find out what they are involves an analysis of the current state. This analysis may use a wide range of tools to determine how effectively the business is operating; for example, business process redesign, internal systems reviews, customer satisfaction studies, and assessments of the company's people processes. Using a tool that identifies breakdowns in communications, interpersonal relations, decision making, and teamwork enables the company's leadership to see the significance of the trust issue in organizational performance.

With the breakdown analysis completed, an additional tool can be used that is particularly powerful—root-cause analysis for people-related issues, or what we call the *Four Whys*. This tool provides a way to understand what is behind the breakdowns in our work processes. If we ask "why" at least four times, and probe to understand the cause of a particular behavior or action, we are likely to find that most of these problems are deeply rooted in the transaction-based way in which the business is organized. For example, MSI's siloed approach to work meant that people in several departments were competing to get the dollars of the same customers. As a result, customers often did not get the information or services they needed and felt caught in the middle.

With the current state, breakdown, and root-cause analyses completed, the team or company is ready to engage the organization in designing the future state of the business and the workplace. The involvement process can use a retreat or workshop format for management and the roundtable approach for the rest of the workforce. Some companies shut down operations for two days and take the entire workforce offsite to complete this work. The result of this process should be a clearly articulated vision of where the business will be once the change process is completed, and which everyone owns.

After the future state of the business has been fully developed, a gap analysis is completed. It identifies the behaviors, processes, or structures that need to change in order to achieve that future state. This step of the process becomes a fairly penetrating analysis of whether the company has the will and discipline to achieve its objectives.

Now the specific change plan, which will fill the gaps, is prepared. It will spell out the goals, objectives, and desired results of the change strategy. It will identify specific milestones and early visible successes that will help build momentum and self-confidence. A set of success measures will be identified, as will a budget, a staffing plan, and an analysis of the return on investment.

Phase II. Initiating the Change

With the change plan completed, the team leading the change process can now initiate implementation in a way that will successfully manage expectations and build value for the change. The focus is on the Will of the process—that is, on building the capacity and competencies necessary for successful change. As shown in Figure 6-3, there are six steps in this phase of the process.

Step 1: Create a two-track process. As the change process is initiated, the ongoing business of the business needs to be managed the same way it always has been. There can be no disruption of service to customers. At the same time, one of the biggest concerns people may have is how they do their jobs, participate in the change process, and also learn how to work differently. It is a difficult balancing act, but it is made easier by the fact that there is a high level of ownership in the change. To manage both, a two-track system of change is helpful. One track is devoted to ensuring the successful operations of the ongoing business. Specific people are charged with making sure there is no disruption. The second track is focused on the change process, which has another set of people focusing on its success. At some juncture down the road, the two tracks will merge. Typically this happens naturally, not by contrivance.

Figure 6-3. Phase II: Initiating the change.

Step 1:	Create a two-track process.
Step 2:	Select your changemasters.
Step 3:	Develop change skills.
Step 4:	Select real work projects.
Step 5:	Protect against early disconnects.
Step 6:	Prepare for the next phase.

The recognition by leadership that a two-track system is essential to success will allay many fears and concerns. It will also make clear that the evolutionary process will go on.

Step 2: Select your changemasters. The change process cannot be implemented by a single team unless the change only involves a single project. If it involves a department, the entire company, or a cross-functional process, there needs to be a cadre of what I call *changemasters*, people who are skilled in the tools and processes of change management. These individuals are freed of their regular jobs to do this work, and need to be rewarded for doing so. There will also be some dislocation that results when they move to their new assignments, which must be anticipated and accommodated in the staffing plan.

Step 3: Develop change skills. To build a level of self-sufficiency for the long-term management of change, changemasters need at least these change skills:

- Meeting design and facilitation
- Team formation, chartering, and facilitation
- Team dynamics and management
- Process skills in project management, decision making, problem-solving, communications, conflict resolution, and coaching
- Change process preventions and interventions

People who are naturally facilitative, or have had previous change management experience, may have already learned these skills. But given the focus on evolving to a collaborative, relationship-based approach to leading and managing, it is essential that these individuals demonstrate their competence in collaborative change skills. For those who are new to the process, a full course is essential for their success. Expect a number of these people to fail the rigors of this process. Being a changemaster is not a right, it is an honor.

Step 4: Select real work projects. The best way to increase the speed of change while going through this evolution is to employ the principle of "real work in real time." This means that changes in behavior, process, or structure will occur most easily when people are working on real business issues rather than some abstract program. If, for example, the information systems group has poor relationships with the production departments, a project team might focus on the installation of a new supply chain technology, with the by-product of the collaborative change process being the development of stronger relationships between them. The team could have members from all the affected departments, sponsored by their vice-presidents. The team would go through the collaborative governance process, and as its specific work began, it would be resourced by a trained changemaster. There would be a definable outcome that was measurable, time-bound, and clearly added value to the business. The project team's results would become a "pebble" in the pond of change. And when the process is successful and replicated, it would build value and momentum for more change.

Step 5: Protect against early disconnects. A "disconnect" in a change process occurs when there is a breach of confidentiality, a leader reverts to old behavior, or a group decides to resist the change process. There is no cookbook to know when these disconnects might occur, but the potential is always there. Engaging everyone in the business in some aspect of the change process within the first year is one of the best ways to prevent these disconnects. It shows a clear commitment to the new direction. A second way to protect against early disconnects is for business leadership to visibly support the change initiative. For instance, it appears on the management team agenda at every meeting. They talk about it constantly. The members are actively involved in team meetings. Thirdly, a constant communications flow enables everyone to be aware of what is going on, so that the change process remains a priority. Finally, nothing speaks louder than success. Confidence and momentum can be built by communicating project successes and clearly linking them to the change initiative.

Step 6: Prepare for the next phase. Since change is constant, the change process itself will evolve as the organization matures. New circumstances will arise and new strategies or tactics may be needed. At least once a month, the team leading the change process needs to meet with leadership to evaluate the strategy, make adjustments, and develop future plans.

Phase III. Building Value

As the change process moves through the first year of implementation, the focus needs to be on building value and producing results. There will be successes, but some level of failure is inevitable. It is critical that the evolution to a relationship-based corporation be recognized as a journey, and that like any long-term effort, there will be ups and downs. By setting these expectations, the value is more likely to grow as the company works its way through the roller coaster of change.

This phase of work involves both the Will and the Discipline of change: (1) the Will because the change process must continue to muster the resources, capacity, and competence to maintain a high level of commitment and effort; and (2) the Discipline because patience in the face of failure, and a high level of tolerance for ambiguity, becomes essential for long-term success. Without Discipline, the change effort can be easily jolted off course. There are, as Figure 6-4 shows, five steps in this phase of the change journey.

Step 1: Open up communications. People need information to function effectively. Without adequate information on a consistent basis, they will do what comes naturally—make it up based on the best information available. This dynamic is called

Figure 6-4. Phase III: Building value.

Step 1:	Open up communications.
Step 2:	Harvest the successes.
Step 3:	Engage middle management.
Step 4:	Realign the organization.
Step 5:	Implement a new performance system.

the "mystery house" effect. It is incumbent on the team leading the change process and management to address this problem directly, not only by issuing a newsletter or communiqué from time to time, but by creating a dialogue with the workforce. This dialogue is based on the principle of openness. The more information people have available to them, the more likely it is they will understand and have value for the change process. Communications need to go four ways: from leadership to the workforce, from the workforce back to the leadership, and both ways horizontally across the organization. In a collaborative change process, there is no need for a rumor mill, nor is there a need to manipulate information. The principle guiding behavior is to build trust.

Moving Beyond "I Don't Know"

In a large distribution company, whenever anyone at either the staff or shop floor level was asked about where the company was headed or what its current priorities were, the answer was always "I don't know." To the outside resources working to increase operating efficiencies, it became clear that it would be next to impossible to grow this business without opening up the lines of communication among all members of the workforce.

Over the next seven months, the CEO initiated a series of roundtables to meet the workforce in small groups, and to listen to their concerns and hopes. A newsletter was created that focused on news about the business, their customers, and their members. All business was stopped for a day to conduct a company-wide visioning meeting so that everyone would know where they were going and how they were going to get there. Finally, the leadership team adopted a policy of "open-book communications," which meant that the company would continue its approach to two-way dialogue using the roundtable format quarterly.

One year later, everyone in the plant knew the company's vision, mission, strategy, and how they fit into it. A workplace satisfaction survey also found that the roundtables helped the workforce feel listened to, and gave them a way to make recommendations for changes and improvements.

Step 2: Harvest the successes. As change projects begin to demonstrate results, it is important to acknowledge the successes and give the teams credit for the results they have produced. At the same time, it is important to leverage these successes into other projects. The lessons learned, the team dynamics that have worked, and the team leadership that has emerged can all be brought to bear on the new projects. At the same time, the team leading the change process must remain vigilant. The members must keep their ears to the ground, listening for disconnects, and be prepared to make the necessary interventions.

Step 3: Engage middle management. As discussed earlier, middle management has the most to lose in the evolution to a relationship-based workplace. And even though middle managers may have participated in the early stages of the effort, now they need to be more deeply involved in the behavioral changes they will need to make to succeed in the new organization. One way to do this is to develop a success profile that outlines the values, behaviors, attitudes, and skill competencies expected of these managers in the new workplace. Then they are assessed in terms of their overall style, as well as their strengths and weaknesses in working with others. A rigorous self-assessment is needed to round out the analyses and to give them a clear understanding of what changes they will need to make. With the assessments completed, each manager will have their own skills-development program and will receive coaching and support to help them be successful.

Step 4: Realign the organization. During this phase of the change process, the gradual process of realigning the structure and systems of the business begins. Everyone in the business is put on a home team. All teams are chartered to meet customer needs. They work cross-functionally and across processes as the silo walls begin to come down. A team-based organization is created. Simultaneously, internal systems like Human Resources and Finance are realigned to support the new organization.

Step 5: Implement a new performance system. There is a belief that people will behave in accordance with how they are rewarded. The new performance evaluation system is then aligned with the core values of the business so that it reinforces the team-based approach to work. A team-based evaluation system is put in place that rewards the desired team, customer, and trust-building behaviors.

Phase IV. Achieving a Critical Mass

This evolution is a journey, not a destination. But one of the interesting things that can happen on this journey is that, like the launching of the space shuttle, there is a point when all the pre-flight checks have been completed, the rocket engines have been ignited, and all we must do is make sure the lift-off is successful. This point in change management is called critical mass, when the change process reaches a level of value and appreciation among a sufficient number of employees that it takes on a life of its own.

Critical mass is usually achieved when about 25 percent of the workforce has high value for, and commitment to, the change process. As momentum is developed, both Will and Discipline are required: (1) Will because the capacity and competency of the organization must be increased and strengthened; and (2) Discipline because the potential for major disconnects and retrenchment still exists as the initial enthusiasm for change wears off and the new ways of working become familiar. There are four steps that can help a business reach critical mass (see Figure 6-5).

Step 1: Involve everyone. As noted earlier, the change process needs to involve every member of the company in some kind of change project as quickly as possible. This is how they take ownership of the future. It means that changemasters are resourcing those projects that are focused on real business results. The teams are using the tools and processes of the Collaborative Method. There is a conscious focus on reaching designated milestones on the way to the future state. There is also recognition of the gap that still needs to be closed.

Step 2: Complete the structural change. During this phase, leadership continues to implement structural and systems

Figure 6-5. Phase IV: Achieving critical mass.

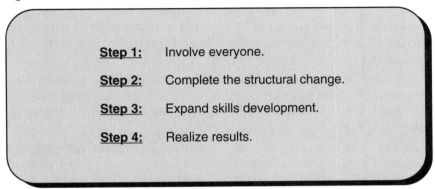

Step 1:	Involve everyone.
Step 2:	Complete the structural change.
Step 3:	Expand skills development.
Step 4:	Realize results.

changes. The silos disappear entirely, and a two- or three-level, team-based organization becomes fully operational. The support functions are integrated into the teams, and the entire business becomes customer-driven.

Step 3: Expand skills development. The skills development process is expanded to include everyone in the business so all employees know at least how to work in a collaborative, team-based workplace. They also need training on how to use the new performance evaluation system. The change masters then put in place a train-the-trainer process to expand the cadre of skilled resources able to facilitate the change process on a permanent basis.

Step 4: Realize results. The goals of the business vision starts to be realized in a significant way at this point, whether they have to do with profit, quality, customer satisfaction, cost, cycle time, or error rates. Similarly, "people" goals are also being achieved. One target is that nearly all of the workforce has value for the effort and is highly productive. Another target is that customers are engaged and satisfied. At this point, profitability begins to soar and there are dramatic increases in speed and trust.

Phase V. Sustaining the Change

At this point in the evolutionary process, the company's return on its investment begins to be fully realized. The danger of reversion to old ways of doing things has largely receded, as both leadership and the workforce become more comfortable with the new way of working. Once again the focus changes to sustaining the change, when Character, Will, and Discipline are at work to ensure the integrity of the ongoing journey.

What this means for the business externally is that sustainable competitive advantage is achieved—-the business is a recognized, profitable industry leader and will remain so over time. Internally, the organization is building trust at the speed of change—it is adapting, flexing, learning, and changing in accordance with the demands of the market. The two tracks of business operations and the change process merge, and change itself becomes the standard business process rather than an intervention.

Change skills are an expected competency of every new member entering the business, and only facilitative leadership are given expanded responsibilities. The focus of leadership also changes from managing the change journey to anticipating the next generation of changes. Leadership can never rest on its laurels. It will always look for new opportunities for growth, maturation, and change. When the business has reached this pinnacle of success, change is a normal part of business life—expected, embraced, and honored.

In Closing

With Trevor and Sarah's leadership, MSI successfully implemented the collaborative change process. They were able to move beyond their past failures, as well as their own anxieties about when and how to make interventions. More importantly, they learned that this process is not easy. They acknowledged the critical importance of conducting a change journey based on principle, and specifically the principles of Character, Will, and Discipline. They learned how to implement the specific steps needed to transform MSI's culture, processes, and structure. They also learned that there are potential disconnects everywhere, and found some new ways to address them.

It is to these disconnects that we now turn our attention

in the remaining three chapters. For no matter how lofty the principles, how effective the implementation, the actual change cannot be realized without going through some degree of struggle and discovery. Those struggles and discoveries happen on three levels: leadership, the workforce, and the organization as a whole. Let's continue our journey.

7

///

Leadership Trust and Integrity

"We tend to grasp for that which we already are."

///

Throughout MSI's change process, Warren had provided all the support and guidance a CEO could. He had given Trevor and Sarah his blessing, made sure there were adequate resources, and participated in many leadership events. But now he was concerned. It had been over nine months since this change initiative had begun. Enormous amounts of time and energy had been devoted to transforming the business. He felt he had given them more than adequate time to demonstrate the value of the change to a relationship-based corporation, but now he was impatient. Where were the results? When would this end?

Warren called Trevor and Sarah into his office, shared his frustrations, and told them he was very close to stopping the process entirely. They needed to show him when and how there would be some payoff and what the ultimate return would be on the investment. "I'm holding you both accountable for this, you know," he warned. "The board is impatient. Earnings are flat. I see process, process, process, and no demonstrable change."

Trevor acknowledged Warren for the critical role he had played to date and then added, "If you stop this initiative now, all we have stood for and tried to do over the past three years will have been for naught. You may remember I told you when we started this collaborative change process that it was a journey, not a destination. Expectations have been raised. The new vision is in front of us. The front-loading has been done. Projects have been identified. Now is not the time to get cold feet."

Then Trevor decided to give Warren the bottom line, but first asked, *"May I be candid with you, sir?"* He saw a cautious nod of Warren's head. With some trepidation, Trevor continued. *"You know where we have come from. One year ago, you stood in front of the entire company and told everyone that leadership by fear was gone, that you had turned over a new leaf, and that this new direction of becoming relationship-based was it. You said there was no turning back. But today there is a rumor circulating that you are going to once again stop this process. With all due respect, Warren, we have a workforce that is still afraid of you and is unwilling to speak up. They don't trust you to honor your word. If you terminate this process now, you will make the cynics right."*

Warren swiveled his chair around and stared out the window for several minutes. As Trevor and Sarah got up to leave, Warren turned, and with some effort, haltingly said: *"OK. I've got the message. I have some work to do. If they don't trust me, my integrity is obviously in question. But let's not leave it to rumor. Please take the pulse of the entire organization. Benchmark our trust levels and the degree of confidence the workforce has in management, and get back to me."*

Warren was shocked by what he had heard. He did indeed have some work to do. He thought he had done everything humanly possible to show the workforce he could be trusted. He had read the books, been to leadership seminars, sponsored the change process, been trained, and helped lead the visioning process. How could anyone not believe him? He knew that organizations do not cause change—people do. He had heard that change began from the inside out, but he had not paid much attention to that. Now he was going to have to go on that journey, even as he faced increased pressures to show tangible results.

///

Organizational transformation is at best a difficult task, especially if increased trust is a desired outcome. But if we have learned anything from the years of change efforts, it is that trust is directly tied to the integrity of its leadership. If leadership is tentative at the beginning or comes from a position of power and control, the change process will falter within months. If the leadership waivers in its commitment during the process, particularly as a result of financial or political pressures, the workforce will take its cue and revert to its old ways of working. Cynicism wins out.

To implement the successful evolution to a relationship-based corporation, leadership must be trusted. To be trusted, leadership must have the highest level of integrity possible— Character, Will, and Discipline. Without that integrity, the change effort will fail. But to break a cycle of distrust and fear, leadership must take a journey inside themselves, a journey that will help them discover the roots of their self-trust. They must look in the mirror, accept what they see—both the positive and the negative—and make conscious choices about how to deal with what they find. One of those choices may mean that they change their behaviors, attitudes, or styles—or that they do not change at all. An extreme option may even be resignation, to guarantee that the organization's change process builds trust and retains its integrity.

Organizations will stop in their growth and maturation at the same point that their leaders stop growing. Change processes will stop at the point where leadership cannot be trusted. Successful evolution to a trust-based workplace requires a leadership team whose members trust themselves and operate from a position of high integrity. It should not be taken for granted. Leadership that wants to increase the productivity, profitability, and speed of the business must itself evolve, grow, learn, and consciously choose to change.

The purposes of this chapter, then, are (1) to understand why business leaders would want to take this journey; (2) to describe a profile of leadership that can be trusted—that is, their character, will, and discipline; (3) to identify the barriers to achieving success; and (4) to describe a six-step journey that leaders can take to overcome those barriers.

The Quest for Trust and Integrity

ent home that evening realizing he was facing a funda-
isis in his leadership at MSI. He was not willing to have
ty challenged or to lead a workforce that was afraid of
new that at the heart of his challenge were his own
, his philosophy of management, his motives for
id his anxieties about the future. There was a lot of
done. There was a journey to be taken, but he was
re about the process or the outcome.

\ ]e?

V   usiness leaders want to take a journey of personal
d⟩   ⟩st leaders, like Warren, have done a lot of things
ri⟩   ⟩ere they are. There may be a need to change the
dⁱ   ⟩usiness, but is it really necessary to change their
lea   es to do so? Is there really any significant value
ad⟨   :ocess if they were to change their approach to
run   iness? Is the view worth the climb?
             : implementation process for a major organiza-
tion   done with much deliberation. These leaders
take   ⌐ ᵤₚₑₗₐₗ responsibility to ensure its success. They may
not be ready to do so. Or they may have a style that will impede
their success. Usually, the incentive to change one's style or approach is the result of some level of pain. But clearly the pain of
not changing one's style needs to be substantially greater than
the pain of changing if a leader is to take this journey.

There are at least three reasons a leader might be willing to
make the change: (1) a significant, personal, emotional event; (2)
a business or organizational crisis; or (3) the desire to leave a
legacy for the business.

A Significant, Personal, Emotional Event

One of the most powerful reasons for business leaders to
open up to the possibility of a shift in direction is what I call a

"significant, personal, emotional event."* Those business leaders most willing to look closely at their own behavior and approach to management usually have had a recent significant emotional event in their lives, such as: the loss of a child; a near-death experience; a serious automobile accident; a major health crisis, such as a heart attack, stroke, or cancer; divorce; the failure of a business; or being fired from a top position. In nearly all cases, the urgency and impact of the event caused the person to take a deeper and more profound look at his or her life, values, priorities, and faith. When leaders look at themselves—how they spend their time and how they treat others—they often realize the fundamental need to refocus. The event is significant in that it is either life-threatening, ego-threatening, or financially threatening. These events strike at the core of an individual's self-esteem, forcing the reevaluation process. The event is personal and emotional in that it involves deep feelings of love, anger, fear, remorse, failure, guilt, or despair. In most instances, leaders find a new level of inner peace as a result, and upon returning to their duties, initiate a series of significant changes in the workplace.

In observing individuals who have actually led change efforts, we discovered a common focus: these individuals tend to be less self-centered, doing what is best for the company rather than what serves their own egos or agendas. After all, they had been to the edge of the cliff, and in some instances had looked over the edge and seen their fate. They realized what was important—that being right and in control was no longer of value. We also discovered that when the going gets tough, these business leaders stayed the course. They would redouble their efforts, spread the responsibility for change, enter into dialogues with those affected, and look for new tools, processes, and methods that would enable them to work through their difficulties.

In effect, business leaders who have made conscious choices about how to live their lives after such events decided to live by principle, rather than by power or politics. Conversely, we also

---

*This section is based on my work with more than 500 senior and middle-level executives of Fortune 500 companies as well as small and medium-size companies in all industry sectors, 1985–1999.

found that when the business leaders driving a change process have *not* had a significant, personal, emotional event at some point in their lives, there was a much greater tendency to give in to the pressures of the moment or to let go of the initiative at the first sign of difficulty.

A Business or Organizational Crisis

Another view is that fundamental change cannot possibly be led by anyone other than a leader who has been through some kind of major business or organizational crisis. Examples would include the loss of a major customer, the resignation of several top managers, the suicide or death of a top corporate officer, or any crippling lawsuit or strike. They are emotional events and are significant for the organization, but will have different levels of impact on individual leaders. Market pressures such as competition or the failure of a product line are usually not sufficient to provoke introspection. Neither is a merger, restructuring, or reengineering project.

In business crisis situations, leadership may seize the moment to rally the organization around the need to reevaluate the organization's priorities. The key difference here, however, is that the event is *external* to the individual. It may be personally felt, but it may not be of sufficient magnitude to warrant a "do or die" approach to change.

Leaving a Legacy

Still another reason business leaders may be willing to take a hard look at their leadership style may be based on their desire to leave a legacy. One type of legacy might be a new direction for the business. Some leaders are able to see where the business is headed, and without fundamental change, they foresee dire consequences; so they set a new direction for the company. This can be equally compelling for those business leaders who, in the twilight of their careers, want to be remembered for a particular contribution. It may simply be an attempt to have their names left in the corporate history books, or it may come from their respect for their colleagues and a passionate desire to leave the workplace better off because they had been there.

The evolution to a relationship-based workplace is not dependent on the leader having a personal crisis in their background. It is more likely to be a successful change process if they have been through this personal event. But it also means that it is essential for the success of the implementation process that we take into consideration the integrity, motivations, and capacity of business leadership to inspire the trust and confidence of the workforce throughout the change initiative.

The Challenges

What does this journey to trust and integrity mean for leadership? For a business leader who has just been through a significant emotional event, the challenges are certainly of a different order of magnitude than for a leader suffering through a business crisis or wanting to leave a legacy. But no matter what the motivation, the evolution of leadership's roles and responsibilities, as well as the emergence of a relationship-based operating system, does require a fundamental rewiring of the leadership fuse box. Here are four challenges in attempting this rewiring.

Challenge 1: Accepting. In Chapter 4, we discussed how leadership has evolved over time from that of having a focus on power and position to that of being a function that can be performed by anyone, depending on the situation. Leadership, in this sense, is based on the principles of responsibility, collaboration, and transformation. The challenge is for business leaders, like Warren, who are in traditional positions of authority to accept this reality. We might find them saying, "I know intellectually that things need to change, but why does it mean I have to change anything in my own approach?" Without acceptance of this new reality, behavior will not change; and without behavior change, leadership will not be "walking-the-talk." That in turn undermines trust and the leader's integrity.

Challenge 2: Giving Up. It is most difficult to give up the belief system that business operates best through the effective use of top-down power, authority, and control. Leaders may have to also give up the illusion that they had any power or control in the first place. This means realizing that the people they work with operate of their own free will. They make up their own minds about what they will and will not comply with. Those of us who have wrapped ourselves in the trappings of power, thinking it made a difference, need only remember the words of one of America's top business leaders, who announced his retirement after twenty years on the executive team of a Fortune 100 company. In response to a question from one of his office mates at the farewell party, he said: "Did I have power? Only when I was in this office. Tomorrow someone else will be sitting here, and everyone else, except for those of you close to me, will have trouble even remembering my name."

In effect, what is being given up is a well-cultivated view that the only way the business successfully moves forward is if I do it. What must be given up is the "I," the ego, the belief that I am irreplaceable. It means accepting that others are competent, trustworthy, and able to get the job done. It means accepting that I am expendable and that the business will go on quite well without me.

Challenge 3: Letting Go. The third challenge is that of letting go. This means letting go of the notion that success is about moving up the ladder, because the ladder is disappearing. It means learning to let go of our distrust of others. In a networked, high-speed world, we must teach ourselves how to trust. *Letting go* means taking more risks, learning new ways to work in groups, learning new ways to make decisions that rely on consensus rather than individual opinion. It means letting go of the paradigm that says control is important, that change is best implemented by changing structures, and that a "just do it" approach produces speed or quality. If we cannot let go of the past, we cannot move beyond our own egos. If we cling to power, we will not devolve it to others. If we do not engage others in the critical decisions that affect our business, they will have no basis for trusting us.

Challenge 4: The Self-Less Leader. The challenge Warren faced, as do other leaders every day, is that of becoming "selfless"—the process of subordinating individual wants and preferences to the needs and will of the group. It means, as one midlevel manager put it, "putting the good of the plant ahead of the good of my department." This does not mean that individualism is lost; not at all. It does mean that self-ishness takes a back seat to the good of the whole. The self-less leader also leads and manages by principle, not by politics and power. What matters is fairness, common ground, and shared perceptions. People know when your intent is selfish, personal, or political. We are transparent. For trust to be built and maintained, especially in a high-speed environment, the challenge for leadership is to keep a clear focus on positive intent—the good of the whole.

The Pay-Off

The view not only is worth the climb, it is also worth bringing other leaders on the journey. The most immediate and permanent pay-off is knowing in your own heart that you have acted from a position of personal integrity and honor. You have looked in the mirror, understood the positives and negatives, dealt with the negatives, and built a reservoir of self-understanding and self-esteem. When you come from your own truth about what it takes to build this level of trust, you are at peace with yourself. Others can see it, hear it, feel it. You are credible. You are trusted. You have integrity. You then have influence with others because you are in a relationship with them.

A Framework for Building From the Inside Out

As Figure 7-1 shows, the journey Warren will take, from the inside out, involves several levels of work. First, it involves understanding the profile of a high-integrity leader in terms of Character, Will, and Discipline. Second, it involves understanding the significant barriers leaders face as they embark on this journey. Finally, as leaders encounter these barriers, there will be a number of choice points which will determine who will successfully complete the journey and who will not.

A Profile for Leadership Trust and Integrity

"Mirror, mirror, on the wall; who is the fairest one of all?" We all remember Snow White's jealous queen, who challenged her

Figure 7-1. Building leadership integrity.

INTEGRITY PROFILE	BARRIERS	CHOICES
Character	**Personal history**	**Six-Step Journey**
• Courage & honor		
• Self-trust &	**Fear**	1. **The need to act**
self-respect		
• Full responsibility &	**Denial & resistance**	2. **Personal intent**
accountability		
• High integrity	**Can't or won't**	3. **Facing myself**
• Becoming "Me"		
	Reversion under	4. **Creating a new**
Will	**pressure**	**future**
• New roles		
• Conscious choices		5. **Competence**
		6. **Honor**
Discipline		
• Choices become		
action		
• New skills		
• Patience, consistency,		
& persistence		
• Self-accountability		

magic mirror to affirm her beauty and power. Warren had been doing the same thing for many years—until recently. This time when he went to the mirror, he took a deeper look and found himself asking the question—"Who are you, anyway? What really matters? What are you trying to do with your life?" Staring back at Warren was a person who had some attributes and qualities he liked. He also saw some things he really did not want to see. He wondered to himself, "What does it mean to have character, will, and discipline as a leader in my business?"

Leadership Character

The focus of leadership character is on being authentic—that is, not having to grasp for that which one already is. But first we must know who we really are and what we care about. One way to define my leadership character is by knowing and being able to articulate my core values. We may have assumed we know what they are or how they play themselves out in our business lives. Five sets of core values are central to leadership integrity: courage and honor, self-trust and self-respect, full responsibility and accountability, high integrity, and becoming "me."

• *Courage and honor.* It takes a tremendous amount of courage to look in the mirror and tell the truth. In Warren's case, his workforce was telling him what they saw to be the truth, and it took Warren's courage and honor to face up to it. Courage is the willingness to take a stand on what is right, and honor is the ability to accept the consequences of taking that stand. Courage and honor are not arrogant, nor are they frivolous. They represent the essence of humility and dignity. If we exercise courage and honor, we open up the possibility of relationship and a profound level of integrity and trust.

• *Self-trust and self-respect.* It is not easy to take a stand for the truth, particularly when it may reflect on us negatively. It requires a high degree of self-trust and self-respect. Self-trust is the faith we have in ourselves. Self-respect is the confidence we have to publicly declare what we know to be true. If these core values are part of our approach to work, we can handle anything.

• *Full responsibility and accountability.* Warren was willing to be fully responsible for his past—his actions, his behaviors, and the perceptions others had of him. He realized he could not run away from them anyway. He could always deny them, but that would not make them go away. He could always point the finger at those judging his actions. Or, since he realized he could not control the perceptions others had about him, he could choose to be fully responsible, listen, own up to what others saw, acknowledge it, and agree to work on what he could.

For Warren, being fully accountable meant he was willing to accept the consequences of his actions, words, and deeds, both good and bad. He did not run from bad news, deny it, thwart the consequences, or in any way renege on his commitment to make things right. At the same time, he did not lie down and roll over every time people said things they did not like about him.

The Deliberate Journey

In his twenty years at his company, the last ten as CEO, Randall had never been confronted with such hostility from his direct reports. Not only was the 360-degree feedback negative, but there were several grievances being filed against him. He did not understand it. The Chairman of the Board called him into his office to discuss his next steps. The Chairman made it clear that Randall would need to take deliberate and immediate steps to address the situation quickly, or he would be forced to step in.

Randall took a week off to consult with friends, colleagues, his minister, and a business coach. It was clear that the data showed he would have to alter his leadership style or resign. Resignation certainly seemed the easier path, but Randall was not a quitter. He chose the personal journey approach to change. He decided to accept full responsibility for his conduct, even though he disagreed with some of the data. It was an opportunity to learn and grow.

Over the next twelve weeks, Randall engaged in a highly structured process that focused on the root causes for his behavior, attitudes, and personal conduct. He completed an in-depth analysis of his strengths, weaknesses, leadership style, and philosophy. Then he began the process of revisioning and recreating his approach to leading and managing. Randall developed an action plan, measures for his performance, and engaged his business coach in an ongoing dialogue about his progress and performance.

Within twelve months, the 360-degree feedback showed a business leader who had regained the respect of his direct reports, a 50 percent increase in his approval ratings, and a business that was on the mend.

• *High integrity.* To have high integrity means that Warren is trusted. It means he has a well-developed set of principles and values to live by. It means he walks the talk, and when the going gets tough, he is willing to be fully responsible and accountable.

Business leaders with high integrity are not swayed by the passion of politics or power, or by appeals to personal persuasion. Their only intent is to do what is right for the business and the customers, even if that means personal sacrifice. As a result these leaders are credible, trusted, and respected by others.

• *Becoming "me."* When Warren stopped trying to prove how important and powerful he was to his colleagues, he moved into a different relationship with himself and the business. By looking hard in the mirror, listening, clarifying his core values, and being fully responsible for his conduct, he found the authentic person he had been for years; his ambition had merely covered it up. He eventually discovered that what really mattered to him was the respect of others, being trusted, and serving others. With this new sense of himself, he became an inspiration to his colleagues.

Leadership Will

The exercise of one's Will is the act of making a full commitment to a specific course of action. In Warren's case, it meant consciously choosing to go on a journey of self-discovery so that he would understand why his workforce no longer trusted him. But the exercise of one's will requires the willingness to take a hard look at yourself. If the willingness is only half-hearted, the journey will be short-lived. There must be a full commitment. Oftentimes, the leader's willingness is contingent, depending upon the nature of the new roles they will have.

• *New roles and responsibilities.* Warren knew when he began the journey that the rules of business had significantly changed. Increased speed meant new roles and responsibilities, especially since his commitment was for MSI to become relationship-based. Warren learned, through discovery, that relationship-based leaders are selfless rather than selfish. Their intent is what is best for the company and the customer. They believe that the workforce wants to contribute and win. So they have little need for traditional power and control. They serve others. They give rather than take. They ask rather than tell. They engage rather than dictate. Relationship-based leaders inspire, provide hope, and share their enthusiasm for the future. They facilitate, mediate, and coach people. They are catalysts for change, champions of learning, and sponsors of collaborative approaches to work. But more than anything else, they work diligently to build and maintain trust and respect across the organization.

- *Conscious choices along the way.* Warren knew that his initial willingness and commitment to this journey were not enough. Given the challenges he faced, he knew he would also have to make many conscious choices along the way. These choices require the leader to go into a situation with open eyes, being aware of the options, the principles upon which a decision will be made, and being fully responsible for the decision once it is made. Conscious choices are not necessarily strategic events. They happen daily, even hourly, when a team, department, or entire company is going through a fundamental change.

Leadership Discipline

Warren knew that no matter how conscious his choices were, it would make little difference to the business if there were no discipline in their implementation. Leadership discipline is often a direct reflection of personal integrity. It is in the implementation process that we find out if what we say and what we do are the same thing. Leadership discipline requires not only commitment and focus but also action, systems, measures, and learning. There are four additional elements: choices become action; new skills; patience, consistency, and persistence; and self-accountability.

- *Choices become action.* Based on positive values and conscious choices, leadership discipline is about the implementation of those choices, turning them into actions that can be owned by the workforce. There is as much focus on maintaining an open process as there is on producing efficient results. There is a commitment to put the support systems in place that will support the new direction.

- *New skills.* To ensure that the new approach to leading and managing a relationship-based workplace is effectively implemented, leadership will need to learn new skill sets, as described earlier. They include leading meetings, facilitation, team development, organizational development, and change management.

• *Patience, consistency, and persistence.* No change process worth its salt will be trouble-free. In fact, if you don't rock the boat, you may not be achieving true change. When this happens, however, the true spirit of leadership discipline emerges—or it doesn't. When the change process faces adversity, resistance, skepticism, or looks like it is going to derail, leadership discipline is tested. The following qualities separate the successful from the unsuccessful leadership:

• There is patience in the face of the unwillingness to wait.
• There is a consistent application of principles and core values to every twist and turn in the change process.
• There is persistence in the face of overwhelming pressure to quit. Persistence takes the courage of one's convictions, an open mind to create new approaches and finding new ways to meet the challenges, and a strong heart to see the process through its darkest moments.

• *Self-accountability.* There is an understanding of the risk involved when a business begins to evolve from a culture of fear to one of trust. Along the way there are successes as well as blind alleys, land mines, and failures. Leadership discipline means that individuals willingly accept accountability for whatever the outcomes. The issue here is not about blame or fault, but about learning, improvement, and growth.

Trust comes from integrity. This framework for high-integrity leadership raises the bar on what is expected of tomorrow's business leaders. The critical attributes of leadership: Character, Will, and Discipline, and how they are adopted and adapted by each leader, will determine the degree to which the evolution of their organizations is successful. There are many barriers that leadership will face as it begins its journey.

The Barriers to Success

//

Trevor and Sarah were quite proud of Warren for making the commitment to take the journey that would help him reestablish a high level of trust among the workforce. It was essential. But they were more concerned about the barriers, disconnects, and other breakdowns that might occur along the way.

//

Indeed, there are many points where the journey can be derailed. Some are more significant than others, but, as summarized in Figure 7-1, the following five categories of breakdowns seem to occur most often and have significant potential for undercutting even the highest integrity change process: (1) the individual leader's history and background; (2) fear, which comes in all shapes and sizes; (3) denial and resistance to dealing with what is seen in the mirror; (4) a negative attitude of "can't or won't"; and (5) reversion behavior when the leader is under pressure.

Personal History

Each one of us is raised with a different value focus. We have each been exposed to different behaviors and treatments, which resulted in different levels of self-esteem. Many of us were raised in dysfunctional families and bring the consequences of that upbringing to work. We have different ideas about what is important at work, the value of people, the value of products, and the significance of process. Each of us has been educated differently and brings different perspectives, philosophies, and paradigms about business to the table. We have also had different worklife experiences that have affected our outlook on the types of change decisions that need to be made. Among the more significant issues that can derail a change process is leadership's level of self-esteem. If early experiences have led individuals to have low self-esteem, the drive for power and control may be a way to compensate. This behavior is shown in many different ways, such as:

- Being the funnel for decisions
- Controlling access of managers to key stakeholders
- Controlling the flow of critical business information
- Getting too involved in the tactical and operational aspects of the business
- Avoiding teams or decentralization of responsibilities
- Blaming behavior and finger-pointing to deflect responsibility
- Getting angry when challenged

Often the level of control and emotion is seen by subordinates as disproportionate to the magnitude of the issue. These self-esteem issues need to be addressed.

Sometimes leaders may verbally support the notion of trust, collaboration, teams, and widespread involvement, when in their hearts they really do not. Open, team-based cultures are usually seen as a threat to their need to control, and within a short period of time, the budget will be cut, teams reassigned, or the focus altered. The result is distrust, anger, lost productivity, and, in some instances, decisions to leave.

Fear

As we discovered in Chapter 2, fear is one of the more powerful forces driving our behavior. Leaders who decide to take the journey to a more trust-based approach to life may have much to fear. They may fear loss—losing their jobs, losing face or prestige, losing a promotion, or losing income. They may fear failure, getting hurt, or being embarrassed. No one likes to feel like a fool, and if extensive resources are committed to an approach that ultimately may fail, the risk of getting hurt and being embarrassed is usually too great.

A third, more closely held fear is that of being "found out." It is what could be called the "emperor has no clothes" syndrome. The change process might just uncover the fact that the organization is not as healthy as everyone thought, that people are really unhappy, or that money is being lost through mismanagement. This could make leaders look bad, reveal weaknesses in their management practices, or expose them to corrective action.

Fear drives people away from the opportunity to break

through to a new level of trust, speed, and growth. Instead, avoidance, denial, and resistance take over, and leadership work diligently to seal up any cracks in the facade. But since most people in the business know the problems anyway, the public appearances of well-being are seen as mere window dressing, further eroding leadership's credibility and trust.

Denial and Resistance

Denial and resistance were Warren's favorite ways of dealing with what he saw in the mirror in years past. When confronted with dissonant points of view, especially if it came from someone who was not respected, Warren could discount the source of the information. Sometimes, leaders choose to respond with benign neglect or by not listening. Should the issues continue to surface, a second level of defense is to resist the data, claiming it is only that individual's feelings or perceptions, and that the person does not have all the facts. Of course, there is only one set of facts that are correct, so the person lodging the complaint can never win.

The third level of defense is that of outright denial. Individuals lodging their concerns in the hope of receiving a legitimate hearing are told, in effect, to go away, that there are no problems and they just need to adjust their expectations. Another way leaders deny the concerns of their colleagues is to proceduralize the complaints. The issues are put on the agenda, but the leader controls the agenda. Time to address them is limited, and intimidation through anger, sarcasm, or outright threats keeps the discussion to a bare minimum. Often the concerns are coopted by the leader proposing a solution that is to their liking. The point is that no legitimate, open, honest, and complete dialogue about the concerns, feelings, and facts is allowed.

Leadership who deny and resist the concerns of their colleagues or direct reports merely add to their troubles. Sooner or later it will catch up with them, and in the meantime, they have lost the respect, confidence, and trust of these people. The most difficult thing for these leaders to do is admit their humanity, and open themselves up to the understanding and forgiveness of the people they have offended. The worst thing they can do is to up the ante, increase the volume, or become decidedly hostile. Denial and/or resistance derail the change process almost instantly.

Can't or Won't

A fourth way the implementation of a change process can be stopped by leadership is when they declare or demonstrate by their actions that they cannot or will not support the effort. These leaders create a negative environment that will not allow productive change. One way this is often expressed is that the evolution to a more relationship-based approach to work is like "having the inmates guard the prison." There is an unwillingness to trust the capabilities of the workforce to do the right thing. Behind this attitude is a belief that only certain people can make good decisions. There is nothing wrong with a healthy skepticism, but this approach can undermine a leader's credibility.

Oftentimes, leadership is not able to make the shift in attitude or behavior. It may be they are too set in their ways, or there has been no significant, personal, emotional event severe enough to make them reassess their direction. Or maybe they just do not have the capacity, skills, and understanding to take the leap of faith it may require.

Whatever the reason, when an environment of can't/won't takes hold in a change process, the entire effort comes to a grinding halt. The cynics have a field day and the amount of effort it will take to restart the change process is enormous.

Reversion Under Pressure

Senior leadership is always under a significant amount of pressure, especially in a rapidly changing market. Whether it is mergers, restructuring, new competition, or financial performance pressures, one of the more frequent disconnects in a change process is what is called *reversion*. Reversion happens when leadership, under pressure, returns to its old ways of doing things, to old behaviors. Reversion also happens when leadership becomes impatient with, or intolerant of, the perceived slowness of the process. If there are not immediate, tangible results in ninety days, the impatience tends to grow.

The result of reversion is often a return to the command and control as the management operating system. Reversion may happen all at once, such as when quarterly results don't meet expectations, or it may happen a little at a time. Sometimes elements of the change initiative are redefined, new people are put in charge, budgets are reduced, consultants are fired, or key leaders become very controlling.

Whatever the approach or technique, many in the workforce may find themselves in resignation. The initiative may be tagged a "program-of-the-month." The workforce will do what it must to survive. What is lost is hope, self-confidence, and trust for leadership's integrity.

Breakdowns and disconnects are going to happen in any change process. The question is not whether they will occur, but what they will be and how leadership will address them constructively. There are many ways out for a leadership that does not believe the evolution to a relationship-based workplace is necessary or adds value. But when these types of breakdowns occur, they tend to damage trust levels for some time to come. It had happened to Warren before, which was why this time he decided to take another route—a personal journey to high-integrity leadership.

A Six-Step Journey to Leadership Integrity

> *"The woods are lovely, dark, and deep,*
> *But I have promises to keep,*
> *And miles to go before I sleep,*
> *And miles to go before I sleep."*
> —Robert Frost

In his well-known verse, "Stopping by Woods on a Snowy Evening," Robert Frost speaks to us of the importance of the journey and our obligation to complete it before we rest. It is a journey for the rest of our lives, not just to reach a destination.

//

Warren had said he was ready to take the journey. He had asked Trevor and Sarah to be his coaches. As they sat down to map out the process, Sarah was clearly uncomfortable. She had more bad news to deliver. "As you requested at our last meeting, Warren, we just completed our assessment of the workplace. The results are not good. We thought we had addressed most of their concerns, but the workforce gives top management very low ratings. You were singled out as someone they did not trust. Your strength and conviction are admired, but they want to know where we are going, and to know that you will stay the course. You are on the right course," Sarah added, "we just need to expedite it."

Warren sat back in his chair, and once more stared out the window. He felt deflated. He was eager to go on this journey. In fact, he kept getting confirming evidence that he indeed needed to take it. His core values and approach to leadership had been called into question. It was a matter of honor.

He needed either to resign or to redouble his efforts to rebuild his integrity in the eyes of the workforce. Warren was not a quitter. He refused to be a victim, and he consciously chose to take on the responsibility for his predicament, to discover who he truly was, to look in the mirror, and to deal with whatever he found. He needed to be trusted. He had to start from the inside out. His journey had six steps, which are presented in Figure 7-2.

Step 1. The Need to Act

Recognizing the need to act is the first step. As discussed earlier, there are many reasons that leadership may be willing to act, not the least of which is to end open conflict in the workforce. There has to be evidence of the need to act and willingness on the part of the leader to move from victim to choice. In Warren's case, the evidence was the vote of no confidence he had just received from his managers and workforce. It had become his significant, personal, emotional event, and it so affected him that he decided to launch his journey immediately. In some instances, leadership denial or resistance is so great that leaders see no need to act. In those situations, the journey will never begin. Here is one such example.

James was the president of ServCor, a consumer products corporation. He had been in this job for more than a decade. He had

Figure 7-2. Six steps to leadership integrity.

run the organization pretty much with an iron fist. He controlled the board and the information it got. He controlled his direct reports through narrowly defined job responsibilities and trans-action-based communications, and when confronted, he used in-timidation as a response. All decisions were made at the top. During the last two years, he thought that, to be effective, he needed to become more collaborative and team-based. Within several months, it became apparent to his staff that, while he talked collaboration and trust, he practiced fear and control. Breakdowns began all across the organization as the breach in his integrity and credibility became known. Staff filed grievances.

Customers filed complaints. Shareholders sold their shares. James denied there was a problem, that it was just a misunderstanding. The board reluctantly stepped in, and after the investigation was completed, James was asked to resign.

Unlike Warren, James had had many opportunities to recognize and become aware of his behavior and its impact on others. Leadership consultants worked with him. The board chairperson conducted a performance review annually. Plans for changes were to be developed. James persisted in his denial in the face of overwhelming evidence. He chose to challenge the process, thinking he was above it all. He narrowed his options by refusing to come to grips with reality.

Why? What keeps us from having this basic competence? In James's case, it was a fundamental insecurity that had him make his problems everyone else's fault. In Warren's situation, he was unconscious—not even aware there was a problem. Inflated views of ourselves, assumptions, expectations, ambitions, dreams, and ego often get in the way of seeing reality as others see it. Self-recognition requires courage. James lacked that courage. Warren, at least, saw the need to look in the mirror.

Step 2. Personal Intent

Warren had already crossed the first hurdle of personal intent, which was the willingness to look at himself and to take affirmative action to deal with what he found. Leadership needs to move out of denial, beyond the won't/can't syndrome, and have the courage to face itself. The willingness to look is, in many respects, making oneself vulnerable, moving beyond the tough facades we build for ourselves to be able to cope with the pressures of work or to look good. Here are several key distinctions about the willingness to look:

- Being ready and prepared for a process that may have results we may not want to accept
- Being open to hearing things we will most likely not want to hear
- Giving up control over the process and the outcome
- Learning to listen and hear what others are saying about our impact on them

- Integrating and growing based on what we hear and understand

In Warren's case, the key to success was not trying to control the process or the outcomes.

The willingness to look means that the leader may say, "I do not know exactly how I will get there, but I am ready to try, willing to listen, and trust I will be successful." For a while, the world cannot be controlled. We suspend disbelief. We risk. We take a chance on ourselves. We embrace the journey.

A second aspect of this step in the journey is conscious choice. Conscious choice is about looking at one's life in its entirety and seeing where this portion fits in. To make a conscious choice to go on the journey, then, may for some be an act of faith, a fundamental belief in themselves. It means letting go of the past, not holding grudges or being angry about what people have said. It means being ready to take a hard look in the mirror, at what others are seeing. While this may be scary, we need not be afraid, for the only person we will ever find is the person we have always been. It is an affirmation.

The third aspect of this step in the process is that of taking responsibility for our behaviors and actions, as well as the perceptions others have of us. As someone once asked me, "Have you ever noticed that when you have a problem, you are there?" So taking responsibility means I no longer blame others for what they see in me. It may mean reliving the pain others have felt, accepting my responsibility in the situation, and setting it right. In some instances, it may mean accepting the consequences.

Step 3. Facing Ourselves

Even if we are ready, willing, and able, it is still a giant step for us to face the music. We may be known as movers and shakers, as people who make things happen. This process asks us to be humble, to open up, and to explore parts of ourselves we may not know even existed. We are being asked to commit to a course of action without knowing the end point.

Integrity does not come easy. So, facing myself means first and foremost that I must have the will to confront and to address the perceptions and expectations of others, and the truth about how I live and work in the world. This will to confront requires determination, courage, and hard work. This level of Will is what drives us to persist in the face of adversity, to pick ourselves up and start over after a hurricane, a divorce, or a job loss. It is what gets us up in the morning when we do not want to face someone who is constantly critical of us.

A second aspect of facing myself requires me to begin the process of self-discovery. This involves the systematic collection of data about me from a variety of sources—my style, behaviors, actions, and approach. Assessment tools like 360-degree feedback or management style analyses can be taken to understand strengths, weaknesses, operating style, and approach to situations when under pressure or stress. Here I will learn about my "hot buttons," those pressure points that trigger a visceral response and put distance between ourselves and others. I will learn about how we build and sustain relationships. I will learn how I behave in groups and in one-on-one relationships. It is essential that, in addition to the objective instruments, I go face-to-face with the key people in my life and obtain candid, honest feedback.

Another part of self-discovery is collecting information about my past—my successes, failures, and key issues. With a clear focus on what has worked and not worked in my life, I can zero in on patterns, aptitudes, and results, and what has given me a sense of accomplishment. Then I will look deeper, at my motivations, core values, belief system, philosophy of work and family, and reason for being on this Earth. Here I am looking for drivers that will help me understand why I do what I do.

With both objective and subjective data in hand, it is important to obtain coaching and counseling support from a professional who is able to dispassionately help me understand our behavior patterns, symptoms, and root causes. I may find things out about myself that I like, and things I really do not want to know. It is small comfort that everyone has demons, for theirs seem to pale in comparison. But it is in facing my own that I will find my integrity.

The final aspect of facing myself is coming to terms with what I have discovered. I find myself being able to accept all sides of my character, choosing to reject those aspects that do not fit my self-concept, and to rise to a new level of self-esteem in the process. It is in coming to terms with myself that I find my integrity. For I have taken a stand for the truth. I have looked it squarely in the eye. I have been willing to move beyond its harshness. With that level of personal integrity comes the ability to trust myself, and consequently to be trusted by others.

Step 4. Creating a New Future

Warren had taken a hard look and did not like what he saw. He found a pattern of behavior that intimidated others even though he had no intention to. He found he did not listen well, that he rushed too quickly to decisions, and that he had failed to build ownership within the workforce for the new direction he thought made complete sense. Now he was ready to rebuild, to create a new future for himself.

The first element in this step is to create a personal vision. This is more than goals, objectives, desired outcomes, and strategies. It is about who I want to be and the character and quality of the relationships I want to have, and how I want to be known when my work is over. This vision should also articulate how I will achieve my new goals, and how I will handle events that might derail my process.

Warren's personal vision was to be at peace with himself and others. He wanted to be known as someone who served others and was self-less. He wanted to be respected for his talents and what he had contributed to others, whether it was to teams in his business or to his community. It no longer mattered whether he climbed the corporate ladder or made a certain income. He chose to focus more on service and contribution. By giving up power as a driver, Warren was able to recalibrate his behavior, attitudes, and actions.

It is important to write your personal vision down, review it periodically, update it, and wherever appropriate, to declare it publicly. In declaring your personal vision, you make it real. In making it real, we can be held accountable, and with accountability comes integrity.

Be true to yourself. Throughout the process of creating a

new future, it is important to be faithful to yourself and the workforce. I can authentically be myself if I am true to my reasons for being here in the first place, my core values, and the type of work relationships I choose to have. Being faithful means drawing a line in the sand and knowing what is nonnegotiable and what is not. Being faithful means not compromising my core values or beliefs for the sake of convenience, politics, or because I want to avoid conflict.

Step 5. Competence

To create his new future, Warren realized he had to develop a new level of competence or skill. Competence is more than our commitment, intent, or will, however. It involves our ability to articulate that which is important to us, and to communicate it to others in a way that empowers them. In a word, it is our ability to be effective leaders.

Another aspect of competence is the ability to demonstrate new behaviors, many of which have been described earlier. For Warren, this meant he needed to become a catalyst for change, a collaborative facilitator, a mediator of disputes, an effective listener, and a champion of building ownership across his business. To implement his new approach to leadership, he realized he would have to learn a new set of people skills, tools, and methods that would enable him to walk-the-talk, inspire, and earn the trust of others. At minimum, these skills included how to achieve consensus decisions, resolve conflicts, and facilitate effective problem solving.

Step 6. Honor

Was the journey worth the climb? At each step on the way, Warren continued to evaluate the circumstances that got him there and the practicality of continuing. At each step along the way, he found it took all the courage and conviction he could summon to keep going. It helped when he realized that if he did not follow through, there would be major consequences. He could run, like James did, but what good would that do? He could continue to deny and resist, but everyone knew what his issues were anyway. The pain of not changing his approach was clearly more than the difficulties he would have making the changes. He wanted to be trusted.

At the bottom of the struggle Warren was going through was his personal honor. If he ever expected to be trusted again, he would need to stay the course, which meant experiencing the pain of the breakdowns and the joy of the breakthroughs as he looked in the mirror, collected the data, went through the self-analysis, and developed a new personal vision. Staying the course meant that when he was ready to quit, he would think first about the consequences. He decided to keep a picture of Mount Everest on his desk to remind him of the journey he was on. Staying the course also meant forgiving himself for the hurt that he had caused others. It meant identifying all the grudges he held about certain people and clearing them up. It meant creating opportunities in which there could be healing moments—when old wars, turf battles, and misunderstandings were discussed and those chapters were closed.

With the initial round of the journey pretty much concluded, Warren's next task was to remain ever vigilant. This meant that he had to continue looking in the mirror, daily. The challenge was to continue learning and growing. Like an organization that goes through a growth process, leaders do as well. In a time of rapid change, no one can afford to remain static. While trust and integrity are constants, our quest for them is a continuous journey. To help us remain vigilant, we might find a coach or engage a colleague whom we check in with regularly to make sure we stay on track. We can put our own personal success measures in place. We can constantly have others evaluate our performance. The point here is that integrity must be continuously earned. We cannot ever rest on our laurels.

In Closing

There is no need to grasp for that which we already are. There is only a need to join the quest for trust and integrity. It is a journey that is from the inside out that calls us to a higher level of leadership, to be self-less, and to be trustworthy. This journey challenges us to overcome our self-imposed barriers, narrow mindsets, and egos to discover our authentic selves. For when we allow ourselves to have the integrity that is within each one of us, there is no reason for people not to trust us.

8

//

A Unified Workforce

"All for one, one for all."
——D'Artagnan, in Dumas, *The Three Musketeers*

//

"So who is responsible for what has happened here?" Trevor asked the members of the change team. He and Sarah had just walked into the monthly status meeting held with fifteen of their colleagues. They were in an uproar over a rumor they had just heard that top management had decided to refocus the business of one entire division by moving it closer to a customer's plant thirty miles away, and to do so in the next ninety days. The change team was upset because the members found out about this secondhand, even though Trevor and Sarah had known about it for weeks. They felt betrayed. Trevor and Sarah were angry that a confidence had been breached. Was it Warren? This move was inconsistent with the change plan that had already been agreed to, even though it seemed to make good business sense.

The finger-pointing was reminiscent of how they used to work in the past. It also seemed to Trevor as though all the work they had put into building trust in this group had made no difference. Distrust was back. As two members headed for the door, Trevor asked again. "OK, we've got a major problem, but who is responsible for what we are trying to do here? What's happening to us? It feels like nothing has changed. We're at each other about who did what to whom. We are not unified right now. So can we please all sit down and work this situation through? Al and George, would you please come back to the table?"

They did, and the entire team spent the next four hours working through the issues and what was happening to the process. As a result, they realized they did not have all the information. They also realized that now, ten months into this process, they were personally at a greater risk of failing. It wasn't fun anymore, and they were not quite sure what the next steps were. In addition, Sarah and Trevor had shared the essence of their conversations with Warren. The cultural assessment had been completed. They had few successes to point to. Senior management was nervous. To top it off, one member of the change team reported that in two of his project groups, there was increasing resistance. A number of people just wanted to be told what to do. Getting consensus was too hard and too slow. They wanted others to make the decisions for them so they could just do the work.

No one ever said that transforming a company was going to be easy. But as is true of so many companies that embark on a change journey, there is much euphoria at the beginning. The current state is analyzed. Root causes are identified. The future vision of the company is defined. The thrill of starting the journey is enticing. Once the first detour is reached or the second mountain must be crossed, however, then the excitement begins to wear off. Leadership launched the change and now it is up to the workforce to implement it. The workforce is the engine of change. They are the ones who will make things happen.

The fundamental challenge for the workforce is twofold: (1) to become more unified as a group, when for years they have worked in silos with defined turf; and (2) to become fully responsible for the implementation of the change. This challenge is not about forming and managing teams. It is more profound than that. It is about how the entire workforce will step up to the challenge of being fully responsible for the success of the business.

Even with leadership's integrity intact, the true evolution

to a relationship-based workplace will not happen unless the workforce comes together and accepts full responsibility for that evolution. This means moving beyond the silos, becoming "all for one and one for all." It means becoming proactive, trying new ways to solve problems, and learning new skills. It also means the workforce will join the journey. They need to decide what type of workplace they really want to have, and choose to create it, then develop the competencies needed to sustain it. Guiding them on this journey are the principles of Character, Will, and Discipline. There will be barriers and hurdles along the way that can disrupt, even derail the change process. To meet these hurdles and challenges, a workforce, as did leadership, will have many choices to make along the way that will determine the success or failure of the effort.

The purpose of this chapter, then, is to provide a map for the journey that a workforce can take to become unified and fully responsible. First, we will look at why a workforce would want to go on this journey. Second, we will describe the profile of a workforce that is both unified and fully responsible. A variety of barriers to success will be identified, as will choices the workforce can make to create a relationship-based workplace.

A caveat is in order. This chapter is primarily about the *workforce* rather than teams, about which much has already been written. While we talk about teams as a basic building block for getting work done efficiently in a relationship-based workplace, the emphasis here is on the role of the workforce as a whole in implementing the new approach to work. On the other hand, we do suggest that the use of collaborative team processes fosters the level of trust, unity, and full responsibility so central to this transition.

The Quest for Workforce Unity and Responsibility

In the change meeting, Trevor tried to reflect on what he was hearing. He heard people's fear of a potential failure of the pro-

cess and its impact on their careers. He heard how much they had invested in the process, and he acknowledged their commitment to success. Then he facilitated a debriefing process that had the group identify all its concerns—for themselves, their project groups, the workforce, customers, and the business. The results were revealing. They fell into two categories:

1. A lack of unity. *People seemed to be more concerned about themselves and their own jobs than about the success of the process. There was no effort by some people to help others. It seemed as if teams and projects had become the new silos, the new turf. Competition for favor seemed to be high on some people's agendas. Motives were being challenged. Conflict and resistance were increasing. Distrust and cynicism were returning.*

2. A lack of responsibility. *There was a lot of finger-pointing going on throughout the organization. The shift in direction was blamed on management, when it might have been due to limited results. Some people were wanting to be told what to do rather than take on new responsibilities. There was a lot of "I" behavior, with people looking out for themselves first. Skills development was slow. Governance processes, especially their operating agreements, were not being honored. Some people just wanted someone else to "fix it" for them.*

Sarah looked at what they had discovered and sighed. She got up out of her chair, went to the flip chart, and put up five words in large letters:

IT IS UP TO US!

It felt like they were starting all over again, but it was important to make the case for change once again, to define their key challenges, and to look at the benefits of their commitment.

Why Change?

The shift to unity and full responsibility requires the workforce to move to a new level in its relationships with each other, with management, and with the business. Why would people want to go through all the changes, twists, and turns that are required? Workforce motives for transforming the workplace are usually different from those of leadership. But given the transaction-based nature of most work cultures, the rationale for change for the workforce is more often than not defined negatively—that is, not having the current state.

• *Trust, not fear.* We earned in Chapter 3 that the trust imperative is a natural law for the workplace. What is unnatural is a workplace defined by fear, intimidation, distrust, and dysfunction. One of the primary reasons for going through the change, then, is to create a work environment where the workforce can risk, tell the truth, and solve real problems.

• *Included, not excluded.* It never feels right to be the last one to find out about what is going on in the business, or to not participate in setting the direction of whatever group one works in. One reason to change is the high level of involvement that comes with a relationship-based workplace. With inclusion comes understanding, and with understanding there is value. If the workforce has value for the work it is doing, it will own it. With ownership comes speed and quality.

• *Contribution and accomplishment.* Most people want to do a good job. They want to contribute and feel a sense of accomplishment. They want to be proud of where they work, want their businesses to win, and want their customers to be happy. This sense of contribution, however, is difficult to achieve when people are not recognized or leadership takes all the credit. While this reason for change is often not compelling enough on its own to cause the workforce to make sacrifices, without an increased sense of accomplishment, the change process may not succeed.

The Challenges

What does the journey to unity and full responsibility entail? The anticipated changes pose significant challenges to workforce members who have grown up in a transaction-based, power-driven culture. They are entering uncharted territory. It can be scary and full of pitfalls.

Challenge 1: Giving up ego. In order to achieve a high level of unity across the workforce, individuals need to give up their "I" behavior in favor of what is best for the group. This means giving up petty differences and grudges. It means no hidden agendas and reaching out to help others even though it is not in the job description. For some, giving up ego may mean their own journey of self-discovery—challenging their motives, values, and work styles. In work groups or teams, it means putting the good of the team ahead of one's own interests.

Challenge 2: Accepting new responsibilities. Working in a relationship-based corporation and participating in the collaborative change process of getting there mean new roles and responsibilities for every member of the workforce. People will be asked to step up to the plate, take on new jobs, learn new skills, and play the game at a higher level. This may mean volunteering for assignments that require new knowledge, working longer hours, and participating in work groups with a new sense of purpose.

Challenge 3: Challenging others. It is not possible to hide or have a low profile in this new workplace. The norm is high involvement, high visibility, and high accountability. That will make some people uncomfortable. But along with new opportunities and responsibilities come new obligations. One such obligation is to challenge other members of the workforce—to confront them when they are not fulfilling their responsibilities. This does not mean making them wrong, but it does mean urging them on to new heights. Speed in a business can be increased if members of the workforce hold each other accountable for results. A second obligation is to challenge leadership to maintain a high level of integrity. This means holding leaders to their commitments and providing honest feedback on their performance. Trying to slide by simply will not work.

Challenge 4: Persevering. Perhaps the most difficult challenge is to not give up—to persevere in the face of resistance, adversity, impatience, and failure. It is much easier to put the responsibility for business or change problems on leadership or others. The challenge here is to understand when and why we quit, not only at work but also in other parts of our lives. Most people quit fairly easily. On this journey, there is no quitting. Like having a child, we are forever responsible for what happens in this new workplace.

A Framework for Becoming Unified

Like leadership in their quest for trust and integrity in the change process, the workforce's journey, as represented in Figure 8-1, is similar to that of leadership: (1) a profile of what it takes to become unified and fully responsible in terms of our three principles—Character, Will, and Discipline; (2) the key barriers the workforce may experience as it struggles with new responsibilities; and (3) the conscious choices it can make to ensure its success.

A Workforce Profile

Intention

"Clarify your values, for they become your beliefs.
Clarify your beliefs, because they become your thoughts.
Watch your thoughts, for they become your words.
Watch your words, for they become your actions.
Watch your actions because they become your habits.
Watch your habits because they become your character.
Watch your character, because it becomes your legacy."
—Anonymous

Figure 8-1. A framework for workforce unity and full responsibility.

PROFILE	BARRIERS	CHOICES
Workforce Character • Becoming unified • Becoming fully responsible	**Systemic Issues** • Team-based • Assumptions • Pretend collaboration • No one accountable • Group-think	**Achieving Unity: Becoming a "We"** • Commitment • Ongoing alignment • Common team template • Performance review process • Hold people accountable
Workforce Will • Willingness • Governance • Dialogue • Conscious choices	**Workforce Leadership Issues** • Fear of retribution • Just the facts • Competition for control • It takes too long	
Workforce Discipline • Pro-action • New skills • Patience & perseverance • Being self-accountable	**Internal Team Dynamics** • Struggle for trust • When trust is broken • Conflict with leadership • Consensus deadlock • Broken agreements • Failure to communicate **Inter-Team Dynamics** • History • Competition & turf	**Becoming Fully Responsible** • Collaborative team governance • Orchestration • Producing value-added results

Ultimately, becoming unified and fully responsible for the success of the change initiative is about the intention of the workforce. If their clear intent is to be successful, they will be. To succeed as individuals and as a workforce, they will need to reach deep inside themselves to discover their individual and team intent, particularly when times get tough. Is it to gain power? Is it to be right? Is it for the business and customers to succeed? Reaching inside and calling forth that which is most important to them is not something that is done once. Like a marriage, their intention for the change process need to be clarified frequently.

Workforce Character

The first focus of MSI's change team was on the workforce's character, where there are two central values—being unified and becoming fully responsible for the success of the business.

1. *Becoming unified.* As we discussed in Chapter 2, many businesses are siloed, transaction-based, and have a management operating system that is defined by power and fear. The result is disunity, competition, turf, and conflict. A natural outgrowth of this culture is what we call "I" behavior, where everyone is looking out for his- or herself first. People do their jobs and go home, even if someone else needs help. There is little sense of community, but there are cliques and centers of high performance. People are usually oriented upward to please their supervisors, and they tend not to take the initiative for fear of doing something incorrectly.

If the workforce is to become unified, there must be a fundamental change in how people work together. It means giving up individual egos for the good of the whole and moving from behaviors and attitudes based on "I-Me-Mine" to a focus on "We-Ours-Us." This may require teams and work groups to look in the mirror at their behavior. It will most likely mean challenging each other to set new standards. It absolutely means that when confronted with external threats and challenges, the entire workforce stands as one.

The motto of this workforce becomes "Collaborate Inside to Compete Outside." This does not mean simple cooperation in the sense of getting along. It means working through differences, solving problems, and challenging each other to do better. It also does not mean having an adversarial relationship with leadership. To the contrary, it means everyone has a shared intent for each other's success.

To be able to focus on the outside, the workforce must learn how to heal its internal differences, including old history, grudges, rivalries, hidden agendas, and points of view that have become entrenched. As discussed earlier, this means specific work on identifying which issues need to be addressed. It means giving up turf, opening up communications, and building trust in all relationships.

Another way for the workforce to become unified is by actively participating in the creation of a common vision for the business. By having a focus that is greater than the individual, the emphasis is on the good of the whole.

2. *Becoming fully responsible.* Are we our brother's keeper? In a relationship-based corporation, and in the collaborative change methodology that gets us there, the answer is an unequivocal yes. This means there is little or no room in this process for people who point fingers, blame others, or always need to be right. There is plenty of room for people who take a hard look in the mirror, own up to what they see, and work with others to grow the business.

It means that we recognize and accept our personal power in how we work with leadership and others. We are no longer victims of authority. We speak up if we believe that something being done is wrong. It means we challenge, in a respectful way, anyone in the business we do not believe is living up to his or her potential or is hurting the business. Becoming fully responsible also means being a catalyst for change. We will not wait, but initiate. Operating within the collaborative framework of alignment, the workforce will bring issues to the surface, propose solutions, and advocate for a quick response. It is no longer acceptable to simply be passive.

Workforce Will

As with leadership, the exercise of workforce will is found in its full commitment to becoming unified and fully responsible; to do what it takes. Trevor and Sarah identified at least four elements. First, it means a willingness to look at the organizational changes needed, their own behavior, and its impact on others and then to be willing to learn, grow, and make the necessary individual and team changes for the good of the whole.

A second element of workforce will is the installation of a uniform system of governance—that is, how people will work together. It is critical that a consistent template be used across the organization. The template needs to focus on the company's core values, their operating agreements, their charter for the task or function they have been sponsored to perform, and the work processes it will use to complete the job.

Third, Trevor and Sarah found that workforce will means a commitment to dialogue in the fullest sense of the word. By creating open dialogues between leadership and the workforce, among teams, within teams, and across the entire organization, there is no mystery house and no need for a rumor mill. There is a high degree of engagement and interaction between leadership and the workforce. And with communications going in all directions, people know what is going on and remain aligned. They freely give and receive feedback and address issues as they arise.

Finally, becoming unified and fully responsible means that conscious choices are made along the way. The MSI team was already facing one of those choices—whether to proceed in the face of adverse news. What is important at the workforce level is that the choices made are done so openly, that the process of making them allows not only facts but also feelings and perceptions to be put on the table. To succeed, it must build ownership and value for the choice.

Workforce Discipline

Trevor and Sarah had already experienced a breakdown in workforce discipline in their change process. They knew how absolutely critical it was to their success. They realized there were four elements here as well: (1) proaction; (2) new skills; (3) patience and perseverance; and (4) self-accountability.

1. *Proaction.* Not being a victim of command and control means that the workforce is proactive—anticipating issues, planning ahead, raising concerns, intervening in the process, proposing solutions—while keeping the good of the company uppermost in its mind.

2. *New skills.* There are new group and team skills that need to be learned, particularly in the art of governance. These have been identified in earlier chapters, but include facilitation, meeting design and management, team development, and interpersonal skills like decision making and problem solving. Two additional comments are important. The most important skill is learning how to build, sustain, and regain trust once it is bro-

ken. In addition, there must be a rigor about the learning process. It must be continuous and comprehensive. For example, it will do no good if only a third of the workforce knows how to operate in a collaborative team. But clearly there are levels and degrees of skill development that apply to different parts of the business.

3. *Patience and perseverance.* In addition, becoming fully responsible means patience and perseverance in the face of overwhelming adversity, resistance, failure, and even broken trust. Patience means accepting the pace of the effort and understanding that human beings take time to choose to work differently. We must also be patient with ourselves, especially when mistakes are made or breakdowns occur. Perseverance means never quitting. We must remain very clear about our intent, values, vision, motives, and the payoff. As we will see below, we will be challenged to quit at different points in the journey. Perseverance also means we never give up on our own growth, so we continue to learn new skills, tools, and methods. This requires commitment, dedication, hard work, and self-discipline. We will do so because the option of going back is unacceptable, and the rewards for taking the journey are manifold.

4. *Being self-accountable.* Trevor and Sarah were quite happy with the way Warren held himself accountable for the results of the culture assessment. They were not pleased with the way the change team reverted so quickly to finger-pointing when bad news came. They were also disappointed that even when their behavior was pointed out to them, many still would not accept it. Being self-accountable means always being observant about your own conduct as an individual and in work groups. Once ineffective behavior is recognized, the self-accountable workforce acknowledges the behavior, owns it, and does something about it. You don't wait to get caught. Self-accountable workforces anticipate problems and put preventions in place.

Becoming unified and fully responsible as a workforce will, over time, build self-confidence, self-esteem, and trust within the workforce. It is difficult work, as we shall see in a minute, because the pressures to derail the process are enormous. But workforce Character, Will, and Discipline, if adhered to, provide the framework for success, even in the face of those pressures.

Barriers to Success

///

The reports of breakdowns all across the organization began to come in to Trevor and Sarah. They were astounded to find the quantity, breadth, and depth of issues being raised. Trevor saw some hope even in the midst of the gloom. "Let's think of it this way, Sarah. Before we began this process, all these issues were here anyway—we just did not know about them.

///

At least now we know what has been getting in our way." And get in the way of fundamental change they did. These barriers were on at least four levels: (1) at the system level; (2) between the workforce and leadership; (3) inside work groups and teams; and (4) between groups.

Systemic Issues

Every business is different, but the management operating systems of transaction-based organizations are quite similar. The process of evolving these systems toward a trust-based set of relationships with the workforce presents some significant barriers.

• *Team-based, or an organization with teams*. Because teaming has become so popular, most businesses have adopted some form of team development. Usually, however, teams are not universal, where everyone in the business is on at least one team. Instead, they are formed around projects or events. In the project team approach to managing the business, many people are left out of the process, remanded to the world of hierarchy and transactions. Nonexempt employees, clerical staff, and wage-roll individuals are often not included. This sets up the business for a division of the house along pay and job status lines. Sometimes, some departments involve the entire workforce while others do not, creating divisions across departmental lines. In still other companies, upper-level management gets to work in teams while everyone else does not.

Without the entire workforce involved in a comprehensive or system-wide approach to team development, ownership and alignment is segmented, resentment builds between the haves and have-nots, and resistance is created by the process that was designed to reduce it.

If the senior executives of the company have no intention of involving every employee in the initiative within a reasonable period of time, the change initiative may not produce significant results. It is considered a breach of integrity if some people get to work collaboratively while others do not. So there needs to be commitment to full involvement in this process.

- *Assumptions about team skills.* At a manufacturing concern in the pharmaceuticals business, every new initiative undertaken was by project teams. The teams consistently broke down, leaving millions of dollars and thousands of hours of waste in their wake, not to mention a frustrated workforce. An in-depth examination of the root causes of these problems found that senior managers "assumed" everyone knew how to work on a team. They did not. In fact, because nearly no one knew how to function effectively on a team, when these groups worked, it was usually due to their leaders.

There was no team template available across the business. As a result, teams became the new silos, the new turf over which managers and supervisors fought for control. Budgets became the battleground, and the lack of two-way communication merely compounded their problems.

Another assumption is that if we call a group a team it automatically is one. That is not the way it works. Teams of almost any stripe, let alone collaborative teams, are new territory. The workforce must understand that in collaborative teams, the whole is greater than the sum of the parts, and they need to leave their egos at the door. Typically, this does not happen.

Still another assumption is that with the appointment of a team leader the job will get done. They tell the rest of the group what to do. One person is held accountable. The irony is that if the leader has little or no respect from the group members, that job will be rendered ineffective. Most people do not work well with people who tell them what to do all the time and micromanage them. If, on the other hand, the person is a natural leader, the members of the team will be facilitative, foster ownership, build self-esteem, and produce results. The challenge is to develop a common template for the latter approach across the business and build the skill sets to support it.

And still another assumption is that workforce members should only have advisory responsibility, but get the job done quickly. "Get input," one senior manager was overheard saying to his newly appointed team leader, "but don't give them the idea that they are making the decision. They are just advisory." This cuts the heart out of the team's desire to produce. They find out the real agenda within a very short time, resulting in a loss in credibility and integrity for the team leader who played by those rules and the senior manager who set them. Skepticism sets in, then resistance, and the change process grinds to a halt.

• *The tyranny of pretend collaboration.* Many companies use the term "collaboration" to mean that people should get along and cooperate better. We have already made the distinction between cooperation and collaboration; they are quite different. The primary difference is that in a cooperative approach to work, people compromise and work around their differences, while a collaborative workforce works *through* their differences. A second difference is that in a truly collaborative workplace there is a 100 percent consensus agreement on strategic decisions, while in a cooperative organization, majority rule is sufficient.

Another form of this tyranny is when the term is used as a weapon to get our own way and make others wrong for disagreeing. For example, in MSI's situation, one change team member accused another of not being collaborative because the team did not get all the information it wanted on a particular issue. It can be used as a club by one group to judge the ineffectiveness of another. In effect they are saying they did not get what they wanted, or they did not like what they heard, so the other is "not very collaborative." This is a misuse of the term and its meaning as a framework for building trust-based relationships and reducing fear.

- *No one is accountable.* Still another barrier to success is the belief that in a relationship-based workforce, no one is accountable. "Teams cannot be held accountable," one vice-president said to his superior. "We need a single point of contact whose feet we can hold to the fire." Work groups and teams can indeed be held accountable through internal checks and balances, self-accountability as described here, and team-based compensation systems. In fact, team-based accountability may actually be easier to administer than the annual process companies go through at performance review time.

- *Group-think.* Related to this notion of nonaccountability is the view that decisions by groups and teams foster group-think and hence a loss of individuality. In fact, quite the opposite happens. When the workforce feels safe enough to speak its mind honestly in a team setting, their real differences and creative perspectives come to the fore. In fact, it is in transactional teams, where the power of the executive is still the rule, that group-think operates. There is simply too much risk in speaking up if you disagree.

Workforce-Leadership Issues

A corollary of these systemic barriers is the conflict that arises between the workforce and leadership because it is a relationship inherently based on power and inequality. Here are some of the issues that arise.

- *Fear of retribution.* One day after a particularly difficult meeting, Trevor walked into the office of the vice-president who was the group's sponsor. He stopped what he was doing and asked, "Well, what's on your mind? I can see the concern written all over your face. Tell me what you really think." Trevor's response was swift. "Are you really sure you want to know?" He went on to tell the VP that his public berating of a team member for not meeting a deadline was disrespectful and hurt the team's willingness to work with him. Two hours later, Trevor was called into Warren's office for a consultation.

Even when we say we want trust and open dialogue, so often we do not really mean it. This contributes to the creation of a work environment that is not supportive of real change and adds to a real sense of powerlessness. There is no point in speaking up since there may be career consequences.

- *Just the facts.* One way that open dialogue gets stopped is when leadership demands that any concerns raised be accompanied by factual evidence. This demand comes from a position of power rather than principle, and often all the facts are not available to the workforce. Instead, they have their front-line perspective, impressions, perceptions, issues, feelings, and concerns. If leadership disagrees with a particular point of view, it can easily be discredited on grounds that the facts are not there to support it.

- *Competition for control.* When an organization begins to flatten, the managers, supervisors, and foremen in the middle are the ones who have the most to lose. If they do not buy in to the change process, they can become a significant source of resistance. On the other hand, the workforce can use this dynamic to hold hostage middle managers with whom they have disagreements. This debate is still about power, and the terms of the debate must be redefined. There should be significant front-end involvement of all management levels to do so. There must be a level playing field, created with the workforce, where everyone agrees to play by the same rules. Fairness is the key.

- *It takes too long.* In our short-term, fast-paced, ninety-day world, there is little patience for a front-loaded process. Impatience at the leadership level can cripple workforce implementation of a collaborative change process. We already pointed to the time differential between planning and doing, for the space shuttle. But what is "too long"? How is time to be measured? As one member of an oil company's change team pointed out, "You either pay now or you pay later. But if you pay later, you will pay more and keep on paying for a long time." "Too long" is when the process is done incorrectly. Then it increases costs, breakdowns occur consistently, and workforce morale declines.

The workforce-leadership dynamic is a very potent one. Leadership can snuff out workforce unity and full responsibility very quickly by posing any of the barriers noted above. If there is no intention of seeing the change process through, and truly engage the workforce in a vital dialogue about the future of the business, it should not even be contemplated.

Internal Team Dynamics

///

The ripple effect of team issues across MSI left Trevor and Sarah realizing that the culture shift they had embarked upon was far more difficult than they thought. The good news was that the workforce and leadership were finally addressing issues that had been with them for a long time. The bad news was how strongly they felt about them, and their doubts that they could do anything about them.

///

Teams and project groups are the front line of any change process. They have a very difficult job learning how to work together differently without having a clear or consistent template. They have difficulty dealing with history without having the tools to do so, and adjusting to the programs of the month that leadership keeps promoting. Here are six additional core issues that present significant hurdles for a workforce trying to become unified and fully responsible.

1. *The struggle for trust.* From the outset, even if team members have worked together for many years, the greatest struggle they face is learning to trust each other. In most small groups, as already discussed, there are grudges, past conflicts, and differences of opinion. There are also friendships, allegiances, and cliques among people who share similar interests, points of view, or commitments. Not only are there often one or more divisions within the team, there is also divisiveness between the team and its supervisors, foremen, and managers. Sometimes there are individuals who just

want to be left alone and told what to do. They isolate themselves from the rest of the team. Unity is illusive in the midst of this divisiveness.

Most people hold on to their upsets or grudges with others, sometimes for years. Often grudges or conflicts can become "wars" or feuds that get in the way of efficient production or service delivery.

Cost-Reducing Parts

In a fifty-year-old, family-owned, $40 million metal fabrication plant that was growing at 20 percent per year, two critical parts were responsible for $7 million of their income in the next fiscal year. And yet they did not know how much it really cost to produce these parts, nor how to become more cost-competitive. An eleven-member, cross-functional supervisory team was chartered, using the team methodology discussed in this book, and was asked to become a collaborative team, and then to cost-reduce these two parts without changing their form or function—and to do so in ninety days. Two key members of this team had been "at war" with each other for most of the last seven years. In the collaborative team-formation process, an opportunity was created for them to resolve that war. Not only was the team then able to meet the timeline, but they were able to work together in a way that creatively designed products that not only met the market test, but undercut their closest competitors by 20 percent.

Overcoming the past by breaking down these walls through honest dialogue is an extremely difficult thing to do, especially if you do not have the tools, the process, or the incentive to do so. These are very real dynamics in groups of people who are trying to become a real team—one that is unified and fully responsible.

If the team goes through the collaborative governance process and actually begins to function more like a unified team, it can also be short-lived. One reason is that often there is more than one team member who really does not want to participate in this approach. The members disagree with the direction the company and team are going in. They go through the motions of creating the group, and then they undermine it, either by not living up to the operating agreements or by pursuing their own agendas. When their actions catch up with them, they either blame others, divert attention to another topic, run away, or acknowledge that they never wanted to go in this direction in the first place. At this juncture, the team can break down entirely.

2. *When the trust is broken.* A second major issue is when the team will be moving along well and one or more members break the trust of the group. It may be a confidence that is divulged, a back-room deal that is negotiated, a member going over the heads of the other members, or a team member who does not do what he said he was going to do, thereby putting the entire team at risk. At this point the team faces a moment of truth—it either deals with the integrity breach or it does not. If it does not, everyone knows it, and the character, will, and discipline of the team break down. If it does deal with the breach, the team may ask the member to leave or hold the individual accountable in some other fashion. The team's identity and integrity can be impacted.

3. *Conflict with leadership.* Traditional managers often fight the new reality of the team or group by using control techniques rather than engaging the workforce in a conversation about the work. In part this happens because traditional managers have not bought into the change, have not been part of the process, or are fearful of what will happen to them and their jobs as a result of the change. Control-oriented managers get isolated fairly quickly. Those who are confused about their new roles may either seek guidance from their supervisors, struggle with the new roles, or accept the need to learn new ways of working. If they come from the position of feeling threatened or needing to control, they will lose out, and it is unlikely the team will become unified.

4. *Consensus deadlock.* Teams have a lot of work to do here. Achieving true consensus is probably one of the most misunderstood phenomena in the effort to become relationship- and trust-based. First, there is a definitional issue. I define true *con-*

sensus decision making as a 100 percent, unequivocal agreement among all the members on a strategic course of action. Many teams have chosen to define it to mean "I can live with that." In so doing, in spite of their differing points of view, they have consciously chosen to compromise—that is, to go with the majority, usually to avoid a conflict. They will rationalize their decision in the name of speed, enabling the team to get on with the task at hand.

In that moment, the team loses the most important asset it has—creativity and synergy. True consensus is not about reaching agreement; it is about working *through* the disagreements. We become truly unified and fully responsible for the output of a team when we have understood why we disagree, worked it through to the root cause if necessary, and realize a deeper understanding of the commitments and concerns of our fellow members. Out of this understanding usually come new and creative ways to deal with the decision at hand, new options, or new approaches. It is from this shared understanding that synergy is achieved, and the whole becomes greater than the sum of its parts. Teams that compromise with each other by "living with" the initial proposed solution in spite of their differences really sell the company and each other short.

A second major misconception about true consensus is to what types of decisions to apply this rule. Some teams have been known to apply it to every single decision they make, whether it is to adjourn at a particular time or to agree on a new vision for the company. There is a need to make a critical distinction between strategic (directional), tactical (implementation), and operational (day-to-day) decisions. If this is not done, the team can deadlock, become paralyzed, and those members focused on task over process will eventually win. At this point, the collaborative dynamic is broken.

A third issue with true consensus is the confusion some leaders have about seeing consensus as a way of getting input versus giving the members a full say in making the business decisions that will be implemented. When leadership is not truly committed to collaborative decision making, it will make the team's role advisory, informational, or for input only. This undercuts the true purpose of the collaborative change process by not permitting meaningful dialogue, and can cause a breach in the credibility of leadership.

5. *Broken agreements.* Nothing breaks the trust in a team faster than members not adhering to the operating agreements to which they fully consented. These breakdowns show up in many ways. Usually, it is in members not being willing to take on another member in a team meeting when they disagree. People want to be "nice" rather than honest and true to themselves and the team. The result is a rather quick erosion of the integrity of the agreements, and a reversion to old ways of working.

Another way agreements are broken is by individual members privately blaming other members for certain issues. Accusing them of politics, of not pulling their weight, or of not being forthright is a smokescreen for that member's not being willing to deal directly with the individuals involved. The result is resentment, politics, and an undermining of the team's integrity.

Still another breakdown is what could be called "withholds," which are points of view, feelings, or concerns about other members of the team that we hold on to. Judging others in the context of those feelings without divulging them is unfair because the others do not know why they are being treated the way they are. It is unfair to the team because it creates a breach in the relationship. Left unspoken, these feelings eventually erode the integrity of the team process.

A team or work group is only as strong as its weakest link. Or, put another way, it has only as much integrity as the most serious conflict or objection it refuses to deal with. The consensus debate becomes the litmus test for how committed the group is to achieving a truly trust-based work relationship.

6. *Failure to communicate.* Even with the best of intentions, the most effective governance system, and clear roles and responsibilities, if there is a failure to communicate, team and workforce relationships will break down. One result is called the *mystery house effect*, which results in conflict and misunderstanding. In a relationship-based workplace, there must be commitment to an open-book approach to information. There needs to be full information, consistently provided, on a comprehensive basis. There is no "need to know" approach to communications.

Another area where breakdowns occur is in not knowing how to communicate effectively with each other. Most people listen so they will be heard, rather than hearing so that others can speak. Establishing open lines of listening and hearing is perhaps one of the more important team processes once it is up and running. Listening and hearing skills are essential, as are skills in giving and receiving feedback. Without these skills, there will be a continuing stream of misperceptions leading to conflicts. Teams or project groups are the front line and the heart of the change process. It is essential that the change process provide them with all the tools, resources, methods, processes, and support they need to be successful. Without teams becoming unified, they cannot become fully responsible for implementing the change process.

Inter-Team Dynamics

Sarah had just come back from a senior management meeting where one of the topics was the lack of collaboration across department lines. Granted, these lines would gradually disappear, but making that happen was an enormous challenge. Because of their silo-based organization, the workforce had learned not only to respect those boundaries but also to seek protection behind them when the pressure was on. There was no incentive to do otherwise.

As if there were not enough difficulties in becoming relationship-based, the inter-team dynamic is critically important to understand. Even with project and departmental teams working exceptionally well, if the cross-functional, cross-shift, and cross-departmental relationships are tarnished with distrust, anger, and competition, the desired change cannot be effectively implemented. Here are three aspects of this dynamic where breakdowns can threaten the success of the journey.

1. *History*. Like animosities and history among members within a team, at most companies there is a lot of history between certain individuals across shifts, departments, or teams.

Finding Common Ground

In a large high-tech company, there had been a ten-year rift between the head of marketing and the head of training for a critical software product being sold at ever-increasing rates to their customers. Even though the managers were separated by 150 miles, their differences were so serious that their own staffs were not speaking with each other. It had reduced the effectiveness of the training process, increased delays in getting product to the customers, and created an environment where customers had to tiptoe around the politics in order to get their needs met. One of their primary customers finally decided that enough was enough, and threatened to take their business elsewhere within ninety days unless their service quality, timeliness, and cost-effectiveness improved.

The leadership of both groups agreed they did not want to lose 40 percent of their business, and asked an outside resource to help them find a resolution. Using the collaborative method, both leaders met to resolve their dispute during three day-long sessions over a two week period of time. The first session was focused on understanding what the issues were. They got their issues and hopes out on the table, how they felt about their work relationships, and what they thought were the root causes. Between the first and second sessions, the two leading adversaries received coaching on their work styles and key issues with each other. They went into the second session focusing the group on a range of potential solutions, and set standards for how they wanted their customers to be treated. The third and final session resulted in their developing a set of "Operating Agreements" by which they would work together, and a mission statement, which would govern their work. They also set a numerical target for customer satisfaction for sixty days, and devised an action plan that would ensure they reached it.

The two business leaders who had been adversaries then went to meet with their key customers to listen to their concerns and to mend fences. The result was that within six months, they were at a 98.5 percent satisfaction level, and the volume of business had increased by 45 percent.

The key is issue resolution, not burial. So many people try to bury the past, act as if it did not happen, so that they can "just get on with it." This is a serious mistake. It essentially licenses the rift, inauthentically papers it over, and basically tells those in dispute, as well as the rest of the workforce, that you don't have to be honest or resolve issues. You can try to bury the past, but all this does is provide fertile ground for more distrust.

2. *Competition and turf.* In a materials company, leadership felt that the company would be more profitable if it had plant sites compete against each other for performance bonuses. What was learned, with time, was that the competition ended up damaging internal work relationships to the point where members at one plant site were reluctant to go to another site for fear of being hurt. In another manufacturing situation, members of the first shift routinely left extra work for the second shift, owing in large part to some personality differences among the supervisors. In a service-based business, a cross-functional team fell apart because two members' senior vice-presidents felt that the team's mandate was too broad, and that the money would be better spent elsewhere.

We learn to be competitive, but most people would rather collaborate. It is when history, grudges, power, ego, or control get in the way that competition becomes unhealthy for a business. When we compete against each other, rather than against our external competitors, we actually increase the company's level of dysfunction and distrust. Internal competition does not lead to greater productivity—only to suboptimization. As we have said earlier, the objective in a relationship-based corporation is to collaborate inside so the workforce can compete outside.

During one change process, ten project teams were launched simultaneously, but they used different templates for formation and project management. The collaborative team, Team Beta, completed its work first and won immediate approval from senior management for its $30 million business plan. The result was very gratifying for that team, but Team Beta was the subject of ridicule and jealousy from the other teams. If one team wins, the others by definition lose. No one wants to lose. So, while these teams were deliberately set up to compete to determine which team methodology worked best, this approach ended up being destructive of relationships. People move around in the business and carry their grudges with them.

Competition, turf, ego, jealousy, and grudges are powerful forces to contend with in any change process. Between shifts, teams, and/or departments, however, they take on a particularly difficult level of conflict because these groups are separated from each other by time, task, or silo. Their identity is with their own group. When challenged by another group, when there are misunderstandings, or when one group feels wronged by another, conflict increases and the potential damage to the company comes in the form of tension, slow production rates, delays in product releases, increased costs, and reduced productivity. Without a common agenda, a common vision, a common template, and full leadership support, the workforce behaves in a rational way to protect its interests and job security.

Conscious Choices

"We are either part of the problem or part of the solution."

"It is up to us" read Sarah's message on the flip chart. She made the observation to the group that it was hard work to become unified and fully responsible. It was far easier to blame others for the shortcomings they were so quick to point out in others. It was far easier to point to the failings of leadership than to stand up and take responsibility for a situation, whether we have the technical expertise or not. It is in crisis that we most often become unified and fully responsible. Our challenge is to consciously choose to emulate that behavior without having to be in crisis. The breakdowns we have just discussed point to some preventions and interventions that can be made to increase the prospects for workforce success—to make the conscious choices of achieving unity and becoming fully responsible.

Achieving Unity: Becoming a "We"

A company has to consciously choose to become a "we." This means that clear value is placed on unity and collaboration over competition and turf. It means that change comes from the inside out, so everyone in the company is asked to look in the mirror, to look in their hearts, and to see if they are willing to make a commitment to putting the company's well-being first. This does not mean everyone becomes a company person. It does mean that the success of the business takes precedence over individual ego, that we work toward selflessness and look for ways to help each other. There are many implications of this choice that we cannot fully discuss here, but several will be highlighted.

First, leadership has a responsibility to articulate the commitment to becoming a "we," to becoming unified as a company. They must put forth, in a consistent message over time, that the core values of trust, unity, and full responsibility are the values that guide the business. They need to describe the behaviors that will be expected and rewarded. They need to walk-the-talk by having the leadership team initiate the process of breaking down the walls. Most workforces tend to reflect the behaviors of their supervisors. If leadership begins to truly work together, others will follow suit, if for no other reason than it is rational to do so. If internal competition is no longer the rule of the day, the workforce will follow the new rules.

Leadership can change their titles from a functional focus, like production or engineering, to a customer focus, product category, or region. They can change the title structure and become business unit leaders, and everyone else in the company becomes an associate. In addition, they can make a pact among themselves that when members of the workforce come to them to complain about another member, they send those persons back to face the one with whom they have a problem, and to have both of them come back to explain their solutions.

A second way companies can consciously choose to change workforce dynamics is to implement an ongoing alignment process in terms of the company's vision, mission, strategies, and implementation plans. It must be continuous, focus on matters of value to the workforce, and involve everyone at an appropriate level—in effect, making the alignment an expectation, and therefore part of the culture. Other topics deserving workforce alignment include root cause problem-solving, meeting customer requirements, streamlining work processes, skills development, and efforts to increase profitability and quality.

A third way to prevent breakdowns in the workforce arena is to use a common team development template based on the culture-first approach to front-loading a team's governance process. The collaborative team development methodology discussed above not only creates a level playing field for all participants but also emphasizes relationship-based behavior, fairness in rule-setting, resolving conflicts, providing a forum for healing the past, and enabling teams to work more effectively with each other. With the governance and consensus-based work processes in place, and with clear roles and responsibilities for sponsors, facilitators, and members, these teams are efficient, fast, and innovative.

Yet another way to prevent breakdowns is to align the performance review process, professional development system, and performance-based incentives with the core values of a relationship-based corporation. Rather than focusing exclusively on individual behavior and top-down evaluations, the relationship-based system rewards team-based behavior, actions that promote a unified organization, and behavior that exemplifies full responsibility, customer focus, and quality. Performance reviews are conducted by fellow team members, business unit leaders, and even customers. The individuals themselves are actively involved in their professional development programs. The appraisal process provides everyone an opportunity for input regarding those with whom they most closely work; this is the 360-degree process at work.

In addition, nonperformers—those who violate their operating agreements or the company's code of ethics or standards of conduct—are held accountable for their behavior. They are held accountable to themselves, by their team members, or their business unit leader. Accountability may range from a learning process such as obtaining new skills all the way to censure or dismissal.

Becoming Fully Responsible

As with unity, in a trust-oriented workplace everyone makes a commitment to be fully responsible for the company's success, whether that is the change process, its production goals, or quality services to its customers. Here are three additional ways this can be done to reduce breakdowns and increase the possibilities of success.

The first is collaborative team governance, which has already been discussed. The key here is ensuring that everyone from the janitor to the president is on a team, and that each team employs the same template, builds its operating agreements, completes its charter, and develops a working relationship with all other teams and stakeholders with which it is involved. In the process of forming the team, it is important to look for "healing moments" to help the group work through its past. In so doing, it enables the group to take responsibility for its issues, build trust, and move ahead more effectively. Collaborative governance is not something that happens once and then it is done. Like any relationship, it requires support, nurturing, and renewal. Ongoing realignment is an important part of this process.

A little more difficult step in the journey is the orchestration of inter-team collaboration in a way that enables people on specific work shifts, cross-functional teams, and departments to work more effectively together. If the intent of the change is to truly create a relationship-based workplace, the silo walls need to come down. It needs to be orchestrated. Certain groups can be chosen to work on specific jobs. Influential members in these groups who support the change can be given visibility and credit for their work. Structural changes can be made to eliminate the walls—for example, everyone is put on a team. But we also must make these changes while being sensitive to the realities of existing politics.

In a shift-based workplace, this orchestration may mean creating an overlap period of thirty to sixty minutes for the express purpose of communicating needs, solving problems, and clarifying priorities. In a cross-functional, matrixed, or shift-based environment, this may mean cross-training as a way to build capacity so that work groups are not dependent on only one person to do the job. Creating cross-shift and cross-functional teams to work on high-visibility projects requires teams to work through such issues as having multiple sponsors from several silos, scheduling, responsibilities, and setting priorities, and enables the teams to use meeting, problem-solving, and con-flict resolution tools. By taking responsibility for this high-prior-ity project, team members are responsible for the success of the business while learning a new way of working.

Nothing breeds successful change like success. A third way for teams to manifest their full responsibility for the business is by producing value-added results. Whether that is the end of a project, the completion of a plan, the installation of a product, or the achievement of specified goals on time and on budget, it is critical for workforce self-esteem to produce valued results. It is best if the results to be achieved are bought into by the entire work group and that they are measurable. Benchmarks and mile-stones are helpful to everyone in the business in knowing where the work group's is. Open communications and progress reports keep people out of the mystery house. When completed, the work group or team needs to debrief its work, celebrate with its sponsors, and be recognized across the business for its contribu-tion. All too often we forget about the learning, celebration, and acknowledgment stages. Yet this is where the payoff is for the workforce. This is where the group moves beyond "attaboys" and career-defining mistakes, to an environment of learning and growth.

In Closing

So, who is responsible for change? We all are. As Sarah so clearly pointed out, it is up to us. As individuals, teams, work groups, shifts, and departments, we must look in the mirror and tell the truth about what we see, and then do something constructive about it. Then we can move beyond feeling like victims and be-come proactive about our own futures and the success of our businesses. The time for pointing fingers and blaming others is over. Achieving a workplace defined by unity and full responsi-bility is everyone's job—both the leadership and the workforce. It is our Character, Will, and Discipline that ensure the integrity of the overall change initiative. It is this integrity that will allow the evolution to a relationship-based workplace, where we will build trust at the speed of change.

9

//

Organizational Alignment: Becoming an "Us"

"Speed is about trust. Trust is about relationship. Without relationship, we will lose the race."

//

Karen was anxious about this meeting. She had been asked by Trevor and Sarah to facilitate the change team's quarterly review of the implementation plan. Warren was going to be there. She knew they would have to look at speed and results—it was time. She also knew they had just begun the really important steps in the change process. They had gotten beyond the denial and resistance. Now they had to institutionalize the change. She wrote three questions on the flip chart for the team to address:

- *How will we know when we've gotten there? When will we start seeing increased speed and results?*
- *What else needs to happen for us to be successful?*
- *What do we need to do now?*

With Karen's support, the team began to discuss them in turn. By the end of the meeting they had answered the questions, but, more importantly, they had reached a meeting of the minds on their next steps.

The consensus view of the group on the first question was that they needed to have specific quantitative measures in place. They agreed on the following: new financial product development time would be cut in half; the turnaround time on service requests would be reduced by 25 percent; the team-based system would be in place, and departments as they had known them would disappear within two years. The cultural assessment would show that trust ratings had doubled, and people would be volunteering to help each other. The workforce would be saying, "I do not want to work anywhere else. This is the best job I've ever had."

On the second question, Trevor commented that there was still much work to be done before they reached the threshold called "critical mass"—that point where there was sufficient momentum in the change process that external influences could not derail it. Their ultimate goal was called organizational mass, *or that point when there was no turning back. At this point, the relationship-based corporation would be institutionalized, even though the journey would continue.*

As to what they needed to do now, Sarah pointed to the need to expand the number of skilled change resources and to increase their skill levels if they were going to sustain this change. She pointed to the need for increased alignment of systems, people, and work processes with the customers and the vision of the business. They needed to produce tangible, observable results to build momentum, and be able to begin showing a positive return on investment.

At this point, Warren, who had been sitting quietly listening to the dialogue, spoke up. "We have made enormous strides this year. Our leadership is walking-the-talk better than ever and is supporting this process 100 percent. Over half the workforce is on a team and working on change-related projects. The walls are beginning to come down, but we are not there yet. We still have miles to go before we can declare victory. We need to align the entire business for speed. We need to show value. I would challenge us, over the next year, to look for a three-to-one return on the time and effort we have invested in this change process. To do this, however, we will need to remain vigilant. There are still many dangers on our journey. Things are really beginning to turn around. Now is the time to institutionalize this change once and for all. It's time we become and 'us'." The team stood and gave him an ovation.

//

The successful evolution of any business from a transaction-based approach to work to one based on relationships and trust not only requires the integrity of its leadership and a unified and fully responsible workforce, but also needs to be aligned as an organization. This means that from the customer to the front line, the leadership and workforce are on the same track. It means that the internal systems support the values of a relationship-based workplace. It means that a cadre of change agents are sufficiently skilled to be able to sustain the momentum of the change process. At the same time, the business is showing significant results—increased speed, greater productivity, reduced costs, more innovation, and higher customer satisfaction ratings.

How a business achieves organizational alignment while producing results and institutionalizing a new way of working is the purpose of this chapter. First, we will look at why organizational alignment is the critical third step in the evolutionary chain and examine a framework for achieving that alignment. Second, we will describe the profile of the aligned organization—its Character, Will, and Discipline. We will identify the key barriers to its success and, finally, suggest some critical choices the organization faces to ensure success.

The Quest for Organizational Alignment

In the quest for organizational alignment, one of business's biggest challenges is to achieve a high rate of speed without sacrificing the integrity of the product or service it offers, nor the character, will, and discipline of the workplace. We all know that markets and technologies change much faster than people can. Even structural, process flow, or systems changes occur at a rate much faster than people can. But alignment of an organization to a new way of working, while operating in a high-speed marketplace, requires people to change any or all of the following: their attitudes, their behavior toward others, their skill sets, and their approach to getting work done. We know that people change only when they have to or want to. It may take time for them to want to change their ways. So the challenge is to realign the organization's systems and processes while maintaining the buy-in of the workforce to the change process, and also keeping the productivity of the business at a high level.

Let's use two analogies to make the point—a chiropractor and a jet pilot. When you go to a chiropractor, your body is adjusted in a way that brings it into alignment—that is, it is brought back into its natural state in a way that the spine, nerves, and muscles are working in harmony. The way you know you are in alignment is that there is no pain. In this analogy, alignment for an organization is the natural state when all its components are working in harmony, when there is a high level of trust, little or no pain, and when it is operating at maximum efficiency. The skill of the chiropractor and the particular methods he or she uses determine how quickly you come into alignment.

Now, think of the alignment function in an organization as being like the instruments a jet pilot uses to stay alive. Every jet has a gyroscope, compass, and altimeter that ensure alignment of the plane while in flight. As it pitches, yaws, and rolls in response to increased speed, wind currents, and the changing terrain, the plane's gyroscope is a way to measure where the plane is relative to the horizon. The compass tells the pilot where the plane is headed. The gyroscope and compass are on gimbals, and they remain upright in spite of the angle of the plane. The altimeter indicates the plane's altitude above the ground. Without these three instruments, the plane will crash. Like the chiropractor, the jet pilot's training, competence, and endurance determine the success of the flight.

In both cases, alignment serves the function of providing direction, stability, a reference point, a sense of internal integrity, and a way to measure when the body is in pain or the jet plane is not functioning optimally. In terms of the organizational evolution we are discussing here, the business that masters the art of organizational alignment will be the one that successfully meets its mission objectives, builds and maintains trust, and achieves bottom-line results. It does this by having a methodology for alignment, competence in its implementation, and the discipline necessary to stay on course.

A Framework for Organizational Alignment

Like leadership in its quest for integrity, and like the workforce in its quest for unity and full responsibility, the organization must find its own way if it is to become aligned with both the market and with its people. Figure 9-1 provides a way to think about this delicate balance: (1) a profile of the Character, Will, and Discipline of organizational alignment; (2) the barriers and difficulties it can expect on its journey; and (3) the conscious choices that need to be made to be successful.

An Organizational Profile

> "In a trust-based workplace, the whole is greater than the sum of its parts."

At the level of organizational alignment, the work that has been done to ensure leadership integrity and the unity and full responsibility of the workforce comes together. It is at this level that all the elements of the change process must work in harmony and balance. It is a difficult stage in the process. Organizations are complex and hard to control. They are difficult to define except in the component parts, and are amorphous and difficult to guide. Therefore, the key to success is found in how leadership and the workforce create and support the Character, Will, and Discipline of the alignment process. Only then can the whole become greater than the sum of its parts.

Organizational Character

Not long after their quarterly review, the MSI change team completed its semiannual workplace culture audit. The results were quite encouraging this time. Every measure of trust and respect

Figure 9-1. Achieving organizational alignment.

PROFILE	BARRIERS	CHOICES
Organizational Character • Trust through full collaboration • Synergy • Business & people systems aligned • Results-oriented	**Market Forces** • New corporate relationships • New leadership • Financial performance	**Becoming An "Us"** **Alignment Assumptions** • Culture-first • Conduct change with the workforce • Pebble in the pond • Bottom-line results • Change cadre • Journey milestones
Organizational Will • Competence • Change cadre • Change team	**Leadership Breakdowns** • Collaborate or else • The accomodator • Leadership integrity • Reversion/cynicism	**Leadership Alignment** **Workforce Alignment** • Enrollment • Value alignment
Organizational Discipline • Patience & tolerance • Accountability • Evolution	**Change Breakdowns** • Organizational amnesia • Never happy • Rollout failures • Change cadre	**Decommissioning The Transaction-Based Corporation** • Realignment of business functions • Silos disappear • People development system **Sustainability** • Change competence • Constant renewal & realignment • Change management

had increased dramatically. There were no more comments about Warren's management style. The communications process was viewed by most to be open. The team-based organization was operational, and people felt that their concerns were being heard. When they conducted some follow-up focus groups to find out why there had been such a positive response, they discovered a number of key factors, which may be found in businesses that have achieved organizational alignment.

• *Trust through full collaboration.* There is positive movement forward by leadership and the workforce teams in building the common ground of governance, a common set of operating agreements, charters, and clear roles and responsibilities so that the workforce can dialogue on critical issues. There is a high level of involvement on the important strategic issues facing the company. Consensus decision making begins to work as teams learn to deal with their conflicts and problems. Fear stops being a player in people's choices, replaced by an open environment, the willingness to risk, and the ability to make mistakes without it being a career-shortening event. Learning and growth replace retribution. Best of all, we can trust people to do what they say they are going to do.

• *Synergy.* The workplace is one of energy and enthusiasm. People come together on projects, work groups, and teams as needed to resolve issues, work through business challenges, and meet customer needs. An idea bank may be created on-line so that anyone in the company, at any time, can record her ideas for improving the business. The ideas are then evaluated weekly by various groups across the business. Communications are wide open, and the rumor mill has no reason to exist. The prevailing mood shifts from cynicism and scarcity to one of abundance. The whole becomes greater than the sum of its parts.

• *Business and people systems are aligned.* Business and people systems across the organization find themselves redefined in terms of the requirements of the new relationship-based workplace. The redefinition is comprehensive and universal. Every work unit in the business goes through some level of change to ensure alignment with the values, beliefs, and practices of the new corporation. Business systems, including information systems, finance, administration, supply chain, logistics, transportation, engineering, and marketing, are part of the new structure, which is a flatter, team-based organization. Their functional experts sit on the customer-driven production or service units, where they can provide direct support to their work groups.

People systems, including human resources, training, and organization development, become partners with the business units or production departments. They are no longer centralized or isolated from their recipients. Their functional expertise is enhanced by cross-training in the company's products or services so that they can strengthen the bench in those areas. Organization development and change are viewed as a necessary requirement for every part of the business. This does not mean an overemphasis on introspection or process, but it will be a recognized part of the workplace culture.

• *Results-oriented.* At this stage of the change process, the front-loading has been done, work groups and teams have focused on critical business issues. Now there is an emphasis placed on producing bottom-line results, including profitability, speed, innovation, quality improvements, and improved customer service. The balance sheet and profit-and-loss ledgers of these businesses should see substantial improvement. Results are valued and are being produced.

Organizational Will

At this point in the transformation process, the function of the Will is to develop, sustain, and mature the organization's competence in leading and managing its own change process. This competence is manifested in several ways. First, as discussed in prior chapters, the business commits to moving beyond having just a change team to create an internal cadre of changemasters who are skilled and able to work at all levels of the organization. The purpose of building this internal capability is to enable the business to move as quickly as possible toward critical mass and organizational mass, as we defined it earlier. The change cadre is selected for their facilitation, group, and interpersonal skills. They are certified in all the essential organizational change skills. In addition to their regular jobs, they are charged with responsibility to help lead and support the change effort. With senior leadership mentors, they become a permanent change team that keeps its eye on the change ball. They are empowered to intervene when asked or needed. They provide meeting, team, and interpersonal support, and maintain an objective perspective on the health and well-being of the ongoing journey.

As this cadre gains experience and maturity, gradually leadership raises the bar and asks the change cadre to become internal consultants to them and their business or work units. These change experts continue to grow their own skill sets and provide mutual support through an internal network. Through this network they increase their shared understanding of the business, the change issues they face, and new tools, processes, or techniques that can improve the effectiveness of the change process.

When all is said and done, the business has a permanent cadre of highly skilled and experienced changemasters who have responsibility for leading and managing the ongoing change journey of the organization, and for ensuring that it retains its focus on trust, integrity, the customer, results, and speed.

Organizational Discipline

With competence in place, the final dimension of this profile is the organizational discipline that results in the relationship-based workplace being institutionalized. One criterion for success here, as it was with the leadership and the workforce, is patience and tolerance. Even though leadership has been patient through the early crises or challenges, patience is even more important now as people tire of the personal and group work required to keep them moving forward. And since the change journey is not a straight line, a tolerance for ambiguity, even reversion, becomes essential. This requires the steady hand of leadership, who sees the larger picture, reminds people of why this journey was undertaken in the first place, and points out the commitments they made to go the full course. At this juncture, organizational discipline is about organizational integrity.

A second standard of organizational discipline is the increased accountability requirements of everyone in the business for its success. This means that no matter who you are or where you are in the business, every individual and team is accountable for both the process and its results. Measurement becomes an essential ingredient as everyone commits to achieving sustainable results.

Finally, there is an organizational standard called evolution, where everyone in the organization understands that the journey toward trust and speed will continue for as long as they work there. The workforce is encouraged to innovate and experiment with new approaches to increase speed and build strong relationships. The journey becomes the underpinning of the company's culture.

Barriers to Success

"We looked everywhere for someone else to blame, only to find ourselves."

///

The change team at MSI was feeling confident that it had addressed most of the critical barriers to success. The team members knew, however, that at almost any time, factors beyond their control could disrupt even the most aligned organization. They fell into three categories: (1) market forces; (2) organizational breakdowns; and (3) change breakdowns.

///

1. *Market forces.* In a rapidly changing market, one of the most uncontrollable sets of changes that can derail even the most tenacious change journey is a new corporate relationship. It may come in the form of a merger, an acquisition, a joint venture, a partnership, a spin-off subsidiary, a restructuring, or an outsourcing of a group within the company. The first thing that happens is that both leadership and the workforce become more cautious and take a wait-and-see attitude. If another company is involved, the power relationship defines who is on top, and until it is clear how the power dynamics shake out, the change effort is paralyzed. As one business leader said, "Why change now if we may not even be here tomorrow?" Cross-company teams are put together to look at how the business processes match up, where the overlap and duplication are, and how costs can be reduced. This process may take as little as three months or carry on for more than a year.

A second uncontrollable factor is that of new leadership, which may come from another part of the company, the corporate partner, or from a different company altogether. If it is a foreign-owned corporation, the parent company may find domestic management no longer acceptable. Or it may rotate its own leadership through the various plant sites. In any of these instances, the emergence of a new leader creates uncertainty. In most instances, existing leadership also takes a wait-and-see attitude, looking to where the new leader is taking the company. Programs are put on hold and budgets are revised as the approach takes shape. Again, this dynamic may disrupt the change initiative, or derail it altogether, if it is not understood or valued.

For example, in a transportation company, the mechanical support department went through three senior vice-presidents in nine months. When the third leader arrived, at first he patiently listened to the management team talk about its work. Within a month, he had formed his own inner circle, and he gradually began to remove the vice-presidents he felt did not fit in. The change initiative that was building bridges with organized labor was dismantled within three months, and the department returned to a transaction-based, power-driven organization.

A third factor that cannot be controlled by most leadership or the workforce is the financial performance of the company. There may be a lawsuit that damages shareholder faith in the company, the bond rating may drop, or a run on the stock hurts its financial position. Quarterly earnings reports may not meet the expectations of the board, and senior leadership is told to institute cost-cutting measures, reengineer certain processes, or downsize the business. The company's credit rating may be downgraded, resulting in Draconian measures that are far beyond the reach of the workforce. When any of these things happen, the most likely response is one of caution, pulling back, and not being willing to take any risks that may put one's job at risk. In any case, a change initiative's budget will come under immediate scrutiny and may be reduced or eliminated, and capacity-building measures like skills development may be put on hold.

Market forces are powerful barriers to the process of organizational alignment because they are uncontrollable. Furthermore, at least one of these factors is likely to occur in any two-year period. They often come out of the blue and can have an immediate dampening effect on the change process.

Leadership Breakdowns

Within the control of the leadership are breakdowns that can be equally disruptive of the change process, since they involve the failure of leadership. One of the ironies of a collaborative change methodology is that when change starts in a power-based workplace, sometimes it must be initiated at the top, with the chief executive insisting that this change is going to move ahead. I call this leadership dilemma "collaborate or else." In fact, in one business unit that had just begun its transition, the senior manager called his team together and told them that this was the direction they were headed in as a business, and that if there were problems with this new approach, they could consult with him privately—about a position elsewhere in the company. To some, this may seem not like failure, but rather an appropriate application of leadership. However, it may create a credibility problem for the leader, confusion in the workforce about the real intent of the change, and even some resentment.

A second type of leadership failure could be called "the accommodater." Here, leadership, in its effort to align the organization by encouraging what it thinks is ownership and buy-in, allows the workforce to do whatever it thinks is needed to begin making changes. The methodology is set aside in the interest of the urgent need to doing something. The template is considered too time-consuming, and discipline begins to break down. Without results or a consistent application of the methodology, the change process can backfire, and the change process will be derailed.

A third type of leadership failure, also discussed earlier in Chapter 7, is when there is a breakdown in leadership integrity. The breakdown may be limited to the change process, or may be entirely unrelated to change or the business. If there is a perceived or actual breach in leadership's integrity, its credibility plummets quickly, and few if any will follow them. But other than breaches of ethics or professional conduct, the integrity issue that creates the most serious problems for the change effort is when leadership does not walk the talk. They may decide not to participate. They may sponsor teams, but then second-guess the results. They may reduce resources, unilaterally change direction, or engage in politics to alter the course of the process. In these instances, the trust is broken, and alignment becomes impossible to achieve.

A fourth type of leadership failure is when they revert or become cynical. Remember that Warren made a remarkable turn-around when he received some very negative, company-wide data about his leadership style. He could just as easily have become negative himself, thrown up his hands, condemned the change process as opening up a can of worms he did not care to open, and shut down the entire process. As one business leader was known to say, "If it isn't bleeding, leave it alone. If it is bleeding, get rid of it."

Another way some leaders deal with negative feedback, or even poor change performance, is to opt out of the process alto-gether, giving the responsibility for its implementation to the second tier of leadership. In both instances, cynicism becomes the order of the day among the workforce, and the change pro-cess gradually loses its energy.

As with market forces, leadership breakdowns are powerful, and are more likely than not to undercut the process of organiza-tional alignment, as well as the capability of the change initia-tive to continue.

Change Breakdowns

Change processes are subject to a wide variety of internal breakdowns, many of which have already been discussed. There are four others, however, that need to be mentioned, each of which can derail the organizational alignment process.

One of the more intriguing change breakdowns is called "or-ganizational amnesia." A company has a compelling need to make a change, documents the cost of the issues it is facing, sets a clear direction for where the business wants to go, and launches the initiative. Then, six to twelve months later, man-agement seems to forget its reasons for doing so, or the severity of its concerns. During that time frame, even with the best docu-mentation, there may be changes on the leadership team, major business problems, or a need to alter the company's business strategy.

These events change the importance placed on the change process, usually lowering its priority. Budgets may get cut, people resources may get diverted to the new, higher-priority concern, or the initiative may be delegated down to another level in the business. For some reason, leadership forgets that its new priorities could be addressed more quickly by using the change process it already has in place. The leaders also may not see that what they are doing is symptomatic of the very culture that the change effort is trying to shift. Organizational amnesia then turns into lost energy, and the process gradually fades away.

A second change breakdown is when leadership is never happy with the process or its results. In one information systems company on the West Coast, the merger team had been hard at work for three months to design an integration process that would reduce or eliminate the tension, conflict, and cost of an impending merger. The two senior executives joined the meeting for an update and to ensure alignment. The team members had anguished over this meeting for weeks, knowing how critical it was to their careers that it go well. They thought they had all the answers. In a carefully managed meeting, the results of the process to date were reviewed, forward plans were presented, and measures of performance to date and for the future were discussed. When it came time for the executives to respond, one of them spoke. "You've done a great job here, but I want you to hurry it up, reduce your process time, and cut to the chase on implementation. And, oh, by the way," he said as he left the room, "don't mess it up."

It is not unusual for leaders who are less involved in the complexities of a change process to not fully understand what it takes to design and implement it. They may not know what it takes to avoid "messing up," to build ownership and to ensure alignment so that when the dust has settled there is a trust-based workplace. It is critical that there be more direct executive involvement in the effort so they understand time, cost, quality, buy-in, alignment, and implementation issues.

A third major change breakdown is called a "rollout failure." MSI experienced this as it went from the leadership process to the change team process, and tried to roll out the methodology into the rest of the organization. The workforce let the team know of its concern through the culture audit and change team leaders. Because change processes ultimately need to have the voluntary buy-in of a significant part of the workforce, the employees hold in their hands the final vote as to the success of the organizational alignment process. Many things, however, can go wrong.

One common reason for rollout failure is when the workforce feels that the process is being done *to* them and not *with* them. Often top leadership makes the decision to initiate the change, delegates to the next level the job of informing the workforce, and then issues a series of communications to let everyone know what is going to happen. The workforce is not involved. As a result, it is quite natural that it may resist or not be interested. Without involvement at some level, there is no ownership. Without ownership across the organization, the change will fail.

A second set of reasons for failure revolves around the methodology. If the methodology chosen for the rollout does not fit the culture of the workplace or has no relevance to the real issues the workforce is facing, it will fail. One common method is to use training to get the workforce aligned. Usually the change is not tied directly to real work, so the process is not seen as a business initiative and is devalued. We might hear, "I need to talk to you, but I have to go to class."

If confidence is not built with tangible, early, visible successes, there may not be sufficient value in the expenditure of time and resources. Similarly, if the process does not build quickly toward a critical mass of people who have value for and are leading the transition effort, the rollout will falter and disinterest will set in.

A third reason for failure is when the process rolls out too fast and lacks adequate front-end planning. Trying to do an organization-wide change in three months, even with a workforce of 150 people, is simply unrealistic. It increases substantially the probability of making mistakes. Many people, particularly the skeptics, wait for the first mistake and use it to dismiss the validity of the change effort entirely.

A fourth area of change breakdowns involves the change cadre. The single biggest problem is insufficient front-end training in the competencies required for these persons to be successful change agents and facilitators. Another common problem is companies believe that people in supervisory or management positions need to be the ones leading the change effort. But this is a difficult position for them. In one manufacturing company, the shift supervisors were made "facilitators" of the team development process. One minute they were training their crews about how to build trust, the next minute, outside the classroom, they were writing them up for a job they did not do correctly.

Building Alignment When Jobs Are on the Line

The executive committee of this 10,000-person service business had decided to upgrade the computer system for their 200 locations, which involved the potential loss of more than 1,000 jobs. They created a "transformation team" with leaders from across the company and the country to design and roll out this new system. When the team was formed, there was much trepidation about how to complete an entire system redesign when so many jobs were on the line, while also building enough ownership for the change that the installation of the new system would go smoothly and without sabotage or resistance.

The team went through a collaborative team-formation process, which enabled them to see the power of true consensus in how they made decisions. They realized that if they were ever going to get buy-in from the field, they would need to build a high level of ownership for the change among the very people who might lose their jobs.

Their rollout process was multifaceted. First, they conducted a series of workshops on the need for the change, getting input and perspectives from people all across the business. Second, they established a communications system that included e-mail and a toll-free phone line, and decided to poll the workforce weekly on their views and concerns about the change. They specifically asked questions regarding their approval of the process. Third, they conducted another round of involvement

continued

meetings to present their proposed solutions, and got input and upgrades to the proposed plan. Then they prototyped the process, and asked people at the locations to help. Finally, they engaged human resources to help them develop an outplacement and transfer program to ensure the greatest security in the transition for those who would need to find another job.

The transformation team produced significant results. Within nine months, fully 78 percent of the workforce approved of the changes even though 700 jobs were being eliminated. A business plan calling for $40 million in new technology investments was approved by the executive committee in large part because of a 5:1 return-on-investment over three years. And 90 percent of the people found new positions inside the company while the remaining 10 percent either retired early or decided to find another line of work.

Still another change cadre issue is burnout. Burnout happens when companies give their top performers responsibility for leading the change effort, but also expect them to do their regular jobs. Because they are top performers, they relish the challenge, but within a short time, these people find themselves having to sacrifice time with their own direct reports, their families, or their physical health for the good of the effort. If they continue to carry this heavy burden for a year without relief, serious personal breakdowns, resentment, or internal team resistance will occur. Finally, if the change cadre is not adequately recognized, celebrated, and compensated for its extra effort, there will be little incentive for these people to carry forward their commitment other than to the relationships they have developed or their professionalism. The best compensation comes in the form of recognition and knowing that when the change process is institutionalized, they have a job to go back to.

Change breakdowns are preventable. To do so requires a process that consciously pays attention to the psychological realities and dynamics of large-scale organizational change. It requires leadership commitment, a collaborative methodology, competence in change management, and a clear focus on the critical need for organizational alignment to be successful.

Conscious Choices

"In looking inside ourselves, we will discover our future."

///

To achieve their twin goals of speed and quality, the MSI change team members began to make the types of conscious choices they knew were necessary to align the organization. Their focus now was on business results, corporate-wide unity, and institutionalizing their trust-based workplace. Their motto was "Becoming an Us." To them this meant that each person, every day, looked in the mirror and asked himself, "What can I do today to help MSI succeed?" In fact, every member of the workforce had been given a mirror that said on its face, "Change begins with . . ." Becoming an "us" also meant looking beyond their own tasks to see how they might help others, volunteering for new assignments, and bringing three new ideas each month to the work group or team for how to improve work processes.

///

There is much a company's leadership and workforce can do to increase the prospects for success of their organizational alignment and contribute to the success of the transition to a relationship-based workplace. There are at least five areas where conscious choices can be made: (1) assumptions about the alignment process; (2) leadership alignment; (3) workforce alignment; (4) de-commissioning the transaction-based corporation; and (5) ensuring sustainability.

Alignment Assumptions

The breakdowns we have discussed regarding the alignment process suggest some very important initial assumptions. First, we must start with the assumption that alignment begins with culture first. It will not begin with restructuring or reengineering or a downsizing process. It will begin with a clear articulation of the core principles of the business, and at the team level with a focus on the ways in which people will treat each other—

their operating agreements. It also assumes that leadership will honor its commitments and will act with integrity.

A second assumption is that change will occur more quickly if it is done *with* the workforce. This means involvement in, among other things, the design of the future business and the implementation process. It also means the change will occur in relationships with customers, who will retain and even increase their expectations of the business at a time when there may be some disruptions.

Another assumption is that the rollout process will start small, like the pebble-in-the-pond we have already discussed, and eventually will become a wave of company-wide change. Along with this assumption is the choice that the alignment process will produce bottom-line results, which will be measured at specific points along the journey.

Finally, the alignment process needs to presume, as said so many times, that the change process is a journey and that there is a trained, competent, and committed change cadre with the resources, support, and wherewithal to lead and manage the entire process. There are two critical milestones that this cadre will strive to achieve. The first is critical mass, which is defined quantitatively as about 25 percent of the workforce, with high value for the change process. Another way of defining critical mass is that the organization will continue the change initiative even in the face of the barriers identified in this chapter. Positively, critical mass is achieved when the change process takes on a life of its own, when teams and work groups are initiating rather than waiting.

The second milestone is organizational mass. This is the point at which most of the workforce has a high value for the change, and positive bottom-line results are being achieved as a direct result of the change.

Leadership Alignment

Many of the organizational alignment barriers to success can be prevented or resolved with strong, up-front, and continuing leadership commitment and involvement in the process. We have discussed the integrity issue at length, but at this stage of the change effort, perceptible changes in leadership behavior go a long way toward underscoring the value of the change and building momentum. If members of the leadership, or even the supervisory level, consistently demonstrate their lack of commitment to the change, disagree with its values or direction, and do not respond to coaching, they need to be quickly removed from positions of leadership.

Workforce Alignment

A way to build awareness, understanding, and value for the change to a more relationship-based approach to work is by using a process of enrollment. To "enroll" someone in a process like this means that they feel listened to, heard, can participate, and that they are asked to join the process. It is in the individual commitment to join that people make a conscious choice to have this change become a part of their work life. Passive involvement does not constitute enrollment, which leads to erosion of support for the process. Some tools this process may use include dialogues processes, focus groups, roundtables, surveys, and an open communications process, which together help build an environment for listening.

Another aspect of workforce alignment is ensuring that new entrants into the business have values and beliefs that fit the profile of a successful associate in the business. If there are value disconnects, or if the person has demonstrated an inability or unwillingness to work in a collaborative or team-based way, the individual probably should not be hired. People should be hired not just for their technical expertise, but for their people skills and their fit with the values and environment of the business.

Decommissioning the Transaction-Based Corporation

After the company reaches critical mass, but well before organizational mass, the process of decommissioning the transaction-based corporation needs to begin. In part this involves realignment of business functions to become customer-based and customer-driven. With those functions realigned, then everyone is put on a team, the covenant is implemented, and the process of learning how to work effectively in a collaborative team begins. The migration to the relationship-based structure discussed in Chapter 4 is launched, and the silos begin to disappear. Work is no longer done by department, but by customer, product, or region. With the new structure in place, organizational systems are realigned. Internal support functions become partners and resources to the business units. No longer located at corporate headquarters or in a centralized organization, these resources are challenged to become valued by their business unit colleagues.

Another major system change involves the people development system. One aspect of this is the performance review system, which is redesigned to focus on team-based performance criteria, review procedures, and incentives. Individual professional development is a critical part of this process, but is a dialogue with mentors in leadership, who provide ongoing coaching and support to them. Individual training needs are identified through the review and coaching process, and are factored into a truly integrated training system. Here, the competency requirements of the business—as defined by its vision, growth strategy, and customer needs—are measured against the skills available in the workforce. Gaps are identified, and certificate programs in those competency areas are developed and offered as professional development opportunities.

Because there is little upward mobility in a flatter organization, nonfinancial rewards are much more powerful incentives. The workforce finds its reward in having greater ownership over its work area, increased input into the decisions affecting the future of the business, stronger relationships with each other and with customers, learning new skills, taking on more responsibility, being on high-visibility projects, and, to some extent, financial compensation. The nonfinancial rewards clearly are the area where businesses compete for top performers.

Sustainability

In Chapter 6, we suggested that the last phase of the initial implementation process involved sustaining the change. In terms of the alignment of the entire organization, it means the development of the change competence that is embodied in a fully functional change cadre. It means that leadership and the workforce are involved in a constant renewal and alignment process—that no one takes the alignment of the organization for granted. And it means that leadership and the change cadre are addressing future change issues. They recognize the fragility of the change effort at all times and are proactively searching for preventions to future breakdowns. They recognize that there are new global realities and economic changes that need to be considered in terms of their implications for their customers, the workforce, and the business. Finally, in their commitment to the evolutionary approach to change, leadership shifts from the position of reacting to change to the management of change.

In Closing

Speed does not always mean going faster. In aligning the organization for speed, we learn that it involves clearing away the barriers that stand in the way of successful implementation. Speed means front-loading, making sure everyone is on board so that when it is time to go, the response is instant. In a medical setting, when the doctor says "stat," everyone drops what they are doing to instantly respond to the emergency. Behind that simple word, however, is a shared commitment, a set of common rules about how to work together, competence, skills that are well developed, experience, maturity, and lots of lessons learned.

In a business setting, where rapid changes may occur with a similar urgency, we cannot afford *not* to be aligned. We cannot afford *not* to be prepared. With leadership integrity in place and the workforce unified and fully responsible, the critical ingredient of organizational alignment ensures that the evolution to a trust-based workplace is successful. With trust built, speed will follow.

Epilogue

//

The Journey Continues

This is the journey that never ends. But as Trevor, Sarah, and Warren discovered, not only was it a journey worth taking, but in the Knowledge Era, it may be the only journey that will enable us to meet both the need of our people for trust, and our customers' need for speed. But as MSI also discovered, it is a journey that requires a new level of commitment and the making of conscious choices. They chose the future over the past, principle over power, hope rather than cynicism, and trust instead of fear.

For years MSI had been struggling to find the right balance between results and process, and between workforce morale and the need for speed. They eventually realized they had been looking in all the wrong places for the answer. They had turned to programs, techniques, and point solutions, thinking there was a silver bullet. All the time, the answer was right there in front of them—-their people. What they were able to do was divest themselves of their past assumptions about the workforce and come to accept the trust imperative as a central driver for both morale and speed. They came to realize that the achievement of self-trust was central to breaking the cycle of fear they had been living in, and to begin the process of putting in place a relationship-based approach to work.

They also found that fundamental to their success was the Character, Will, and Discipline of their collaborative approach to change. They learned that their Character was defined by the principle of trust and a clear intention for the success of the entire organization. They discovered that their Will had to be framed by their commitment to take the journey and a willingness to look in the mirror, choose new ways of behaving, and develop new skills to manifest those behaviors. Finally, they found that their Discipline was defined by their patience in the face of the adversity and in their tolerance for ambiguity.

Trevor, Sarah, and Warren also learned that evolving an entire corporation into a new way of working had many levels and was fraught with potential disconnects. They learned that the application of Character, Will, and Discipline to their leadership, workforce, and the organization as a whole enabled them to navigate successfully through these difficulties.

The first level of change was their leadership, whose central challenge was to establish and maintain its integrity throughout the journey. The second level was the development of a unified workforce that was fully responsible for the success of the business. And the third level of change was aligning the entire organization for trust and speed.

In the face of rapid change, we, like MSI, also have a choice. It is a choice to move beyond the tyranny of the urgent and the paradigms of the past. Our challenge now is to evolve our organizations to the next level of human development. Our opportunity is nothing less than to build trust at the speed of change by creating a relationship-based corporation.

Good luck on your continuing journey.

Recommended Readings

Bolman, Lee, and Deal, Terrence E. *Leading With Soul.* San Francisco: Jossey-Bass, 1995.

Collins, James C., Porras, Jerry I. *Built to Last: Successful Habits of Visionary Companies.* New York: HarperBusiness, 1997.

George, Stephen. *Uncommon Sense: Creating Business Excellence in Your Organization.* New York: John Wiley & Sons, 1997.

Gilley, Kay. *Leading From the Heart: Choosing Courage Over Fear in the Workplace.* Boston: Butterworth-Heinemann, 1997.

Gouillart, Francis J., and Kelly, James N. *Transforming the Organization.* New York: McGraw-Hill, 1995.

Harris, Ph.D., Jim, and Brannick, Ph.D., Joan. *Finding & Keeping Great Employees.* New York: AMACOM, 1999.

Head, Christopher W. *Beyond Corporate Transformation: A Whole Systems Approach to Creating and Sustaining High Performance.* Portland, Oreg.: Productivity Press, 1997.

Labovitz, George, and Rosansky, Victor. *The Power of Alignment: How Great Companies Stay Centered and Accomplish Extraordinary Things.* New York: John Wiley & Sons, 1997.

Lucas, James R. *The Passionate Organization: Igniting the Fire of Employee Commitment.* New York: AMACOM, 1999.

Maira, Arun, and Scott-Morgan, Peter. *The Accelerating Organization: Embracing the Human Face of Change,* New York: McGraw-Hill, 1997.

Marshall, Ph.D., Edward M. *Transforming the Way We Work: The Power of the Collaborative Workplace.* New York: AMACOM, 1995.

Miles, Robert H. *Leading Corporate Transformation: A Blueprint for Business Renewal.* San Francisco: Jossey-Bass, 1997.

Reichheld, Frederick F. *The Loyalty Effect: The Hidden Force Behind Growth, Profits, and Lasting Value.* Bain & Co., 1996.

Ryan, Kathleen D., and Oestreich, Daniel K. *Driving Fear Out of the Workplace.* San Francisco: Jossey-Bass, 1991.

Shaw, Robert B. *Trust in the Balance: Building Successful Organizations on Results, Integrity, and Concern,* San Francisco: Jossey-Bass, 1997.

Index